Football Wizard

Football Wizard

The Billy Meredith Story

John Harding

Robson Books

For my Dad, the greatest football fan

Published in 1998 by Robson Books Ltd.
Bolsover House, 5–6 Clipstone Street,
London W1P 8LE.

© John Harding 1985, 1998

ISBN 1 86105 137 9

Photoset in North Wales by Derek Doyle & Associates,
Mold, Flintshire. Printed in Great Britain by
St Edmundsbury Press, Bury St Edmunds, Suffolk.

Contents

Acknowledgements

The author wishes to acknowledge the help given by the following: Mrs Brooker-Meredith and her sister Lily Pringle, Billy Haining, Owen Meredith of Wigan, the Roberts family, Iad Rodgers, W.H. Jones and the people of Chirk; Miss Alison Astin, Mrs Ovendon, the late Bill Miles, John Maddocks, the Williams brothers, G.H. Worthington, Mrs Robinson, J. Fitzpatrick, Wm Stitt, W. Roberts and many more from Manchester who wrote with memories of Billy; Jack Phillips of Weston Rhyn, T. Ceirog Williams, Peter Corrigan, David Whitcomb, Cliff Jones, Jimmy Murphy, Cliff Lloyd; Dr Percy Young, Ken Oultram, Elna Harrison; Ray Goble, John Hewitt, Dr Tony Mason, A.D. George, Chris Makepiece, Stan Royle of the *Manchester Evening News*, Andrew Ward, Anton Rippon, John Grainger plus numerous septuagenarians, octogenarians and even nonogenarians up and down the country who have added a word and a memory; and lastly Janet Unwin for her honest and invaluable textual criticism.

Introduction

The following account of Billy Meredith's life in football over more than fifty years, does not pretend to be a biography in the fullest sense of the word. Meredith died in 1958 and all of his close colleagues have also long since departed. A few men and women who knew him remain, particularly his two daughters, Lily and Winifred, their children and grandchildren. But, no matter how keen their memories, there can be no adequate substitute for the man himself who might have explained his motives at certain puzzling turns in his career, and who could have recalled his true emotions, and provided insights far deeper than any collection of newspaper cuttings.

So what is the point in trying to write an account of Meredith's life? There are several. First, he was such an important player in the history of the game, a giant in terms of prestige and legend, that the bare facts deserve to be laid out as fully as possible. Second, his turbulent career illustrates just how early did the professional game take on the shape and feel of its modern counterpart, suffering from many of the same inherent contradictions as it does today. Third, so little is known of the style of the great players of the past, and through contemporary commentators, a glimpse of the great man in action might prove rewarding. And last, there can have been few players so affectionately caricatured as Meredith, who achieved fame commensurate with the music-hall stars of his day.

Thus, a look at some of the many photographs and cartoons of him at work and at play, provides us with a fascinating glimpse of an Edwardian working-class hero of whom most of us know nothing beyond the name – Billy Meredith, the Welsh Wizard of Football.

Prologue

'I am told that I had not been introduced to the world very long before I began to kick and I've been kicking ever since. When I haven't a football to kick I can generally find something to kick against and I guess I shall give a mighty kick when the time comes for me to leave the world behind.'
Billy Meredith's Memoirs, Topical Times, October 1919

Billy Meredith died in Manchester on 19 April 1958, two months after the Munich air crash and two weeks before the Manchester United-Bolton Wanderers FA Cup Final. Since that dreadful February day when United's brilliant young team was destroyed in the ice and slush and tangled metal at the end of an airport runway, the front pages of a nation's newspapers had been dominated by the life-and-death struggles of Duncan Edwards, Johnny Berry and Matt Busby, while the sports pages had chronicled the breathless, bizarre progress of Jimmy Murphy's makeshift United side towards Wembley.

On 19 April itself, Matt Busby was preparing to leave the Munich hospital and return to Manchester; on that very afternoon Bobby Charlton (who had been thrown clear of the crashing aeroplane still strapped to his seat) was making his England debut at Hampden Park. These were living legends, while the dead – some barely out of their teens – had been buried amid incredible scenes as workers defied bosses to leave their factories and watch the passing corteges.

Thus, the announcement of Billy Meredith's death at the age of eighty-three, though not unnoticed, could only be briefly acknowledged – the public were looking elsewhere. At his funeral, barely one hundred turned up to pay their respects; only in Chirk, his birthplace, were black arm-bands worn during an insignificant Welsh Junior Cup match, and the *Last Post* sounded.

But Billy Meredith was as much a football folk-hero as the young men who had perished at Munich and, strangely, his name is just as fresh and bright today as it was twenty-five, fifty, even ninety years ago. Strangely, because there can be no-one alive today who saw him play in his prime, only a few perhaps who witnessed his incredible football finale in the early 1920s. Apart from his Cup Final shirt on display in Manchester United's Museum, the only visible memorial to him in Manchester, the city whose early football name he helped to make, is a Billy Meredith Close near the Maine Road stadium, one of several streets named after former City stars.

The puzzle of his enduring fame has no easy answer; most of the great footballers of Meredith's day are now completely forgotten. Who, beyond a learned few, can speak of Athersmith, Bassett, Templeton and Bridgett? In similar fashion, though more sadly, who speaks of Pegg, Whelan, and Jones who died at Munich alongside the immortal Edwards? Sudden death can sometimes create a legend; more often, however, it is a process of deeper memories surfacing in time of need, of embroidered, yet essential recollections, of stubborn images that refuse to fade.

Thus, Billy Meredith's unregarded passing has had no bearing on his subsequent enduring fame. It was as though he had momentarily side-stepped us all – slipped past the floundering full-back and had gone before we had time to look up.

Yet he is destined to reappear, time and time again, swiftly and mysteriously, to deliver his mighty kick with unerring aim. . .

A GREAT WELSHMAN.

SPORTSMEN are a superstitious race. They believe in omens, signs, and the like. Should a cricketer drop his bat on the way to the wicket he is uneasy. Should a football team pass a funeral cortege they at once have forebodings as to their fate for the day. So I was able to understand William Meredith, the great Association football player and Welsh multi-internationals, when he said to me, "I was born to play football, you know." And William the Conqueror, as he has been named, has played for all the world as though he were specially designed for the game, showing marvellous form year in, year out, without ever experiencing injury or loss of pace. It is certain that his superior has never been seen, and it is a great question whether Isiah Bassett was quite his equal as a craftsman with the ball.

The public, of course, know all about Meredith's prowess, and I am going to say little on that head. Rather do I intend to deal with the private life of the great athlete, and that side of his career of which the thousands interested in him know little.

The Two Merediths.

Like all great men, Meredith has peculiarities. There are two Merediths whom I know. One is the quiet, keen, business man behind the counter, and the other the Manchester United football player, brimful of boyish fun, silly pranks, practical jokes, and athletic enthusiasm.

There never were two such opposite characters as Meredith, of Friday, in the shop, and Meredith, of Saturday, in the railway saloon. Grave and sedate behind the counter on Friday morning, on the same night in some far-distant hotel he will occupy himself with pulling the laces from out of his comrades' boots, and in the morning, with a face that is childlike and bland, will sympathise and say harsh things about the villain guilty of so unkind and troublesome an act.

Perhaps the chief characteristic of this great footballer and keen business man is his determination to prosper in the world, and his realisation of his citizen responsibilities. There be those who sneer at this trait in his character, but they be fools, and the man at whom they sneer is surely wise. Meredith thinks that a man who plays professional football should be a good and prosperous citizen, and such he intends to be. No sensible person would blame him for that. So, his leisure hours are passed in his shop, and when playing days are old he will not be, as many before him have been, a man with naught of which to boast, save memories and sad reflections on the eternal "what might have been."

A peculiar thing about the great Welsh football player is his own flesh. No player ever had flesh that would last so rapidly. Cuts and bruises that would last for days on others are better in a few hours on Meredith, a fact for which he is devoutly thankful.

A man whose only luxuries are an occasional glass of claret and a pipe, who spares no pains to keep himself fit, and who glories in his own fame, Meredith is such a professional as any club might

people through the turnstiles. Finally, he led them to a Cup Final triumph, and last season he played a great part in the winning of the League Championship by Manchester United. Colin Veitch, the Newcastle United captain, once said to the writer: "Meredith, on his day, can carry a forward line along himself"—a great tribute from a great player.

It is well known that there are people who sneer at the paid player, asserting that so soon as a man is paid for playing a game he loses enthusiasm, interest, and sportsmanship. I should like some

disciple of this absurd creed to meet Meredith. It would be a revelation to him. The Welshman has been playing in League football since 1895, and has now taken part in 28 international games, yet to-day he is better than ever, and keener than ever. He talks football as though it were the sole thing of interest in the world, and no man is happier than he on the eve of a big game.

He makes no secret of the fact that he believes that the clubs make a mistake in refusing to allow players to follow employment. When first he played for Manchester City he worked in the pits of Chirk, and once he worked all Friday and right through the night, played in Manchester on Saturday afternoon, and was down the pit again the same night,

the freaks of Fortune.
argument.

Few people know that M few yards inside the Welsh by error, he was selected to

While playing against N season he scored his 200th fact seeing that his first sphere, years before, wa same club.

Only three half-backs have of being able to hold him Heath), Bla and Lintott played for F last season. so closely t annoyed, and lish goal wen of dark disas Leek the We the young a for a bit an Lintott's nai sorry, but I here." Willi story with gr

Some Weak

In all the never been b tribute to hi see him drib with one ey other on the latter's out right second

Like most and he is a afraid. As a not bear to All his life success. He with Manche all the years never had or one with his can be no d days Wales testimonial f player.

I have me practical jok an Austrian Bannister, could do eve he first turn United 100,0 ground and mission outs into the col tion.

Meredith i not speak fluently, and how at half national game at Wrexha whom he did not know, d room, shook his hand, Meredith did not understa his idol could not speak stranger rose and marche out of the room.

Just another story in o nothing if not a keen be Austria a wealthy admir would like something to n by. Meredith sold the mi be such—his football boots

If, at the Welsh Eisteddfod, they had prize for
skilful feet, what a strong chance the owner of the
above would have.

1

A Boy from Chirk

'I could not help remarking when I renewed acquaintance with Billy Meredith at Cardiff what little change I found in him. His once black hair is tinged with grey; tell-tale lines have eaten into his typical Welsh face, but he has still the trim figure of a sprinter. It is more than thirty years since I first met William of the bandy legs. He was decidedly Chirk then; he is still Chirk, and if he ever effects any other head-gear than a cap, or decides not to stow away his hands in his trouser-pockets after the manner of the boys in the village, he will cease to be Meredith. And he will alter impossibly if he isn't forever regretting to the end of his days that he is not chasing the big ball.'
Topical Times, 14 November 1925.

Billy Meredith grew up in the small Denbighshire village of Chirk, a few hundred yards inside Wales on the Shropshire border. In July 1894, the *Border Counties Advertiser*, in describing the sixty-eighth anniversary celebrations of the Chirk Union Friendly Society, spoke of banners fluttering in bright sunshine, the Union Jack flying from the tower of the Old Parish Church, and the music of the band playing as the celebrants paraded around the village green. The appearance of the 'pretty little village of Chirk' was one of 'high festivity'.

The idyllic rural setting is deceptive however. When Meredith was born, in July 1874, the gentle valley stretching south from Wrexham along the River Dee was the heart of an important coal-mining area supplying the ever-expanding industrial sprawl of Lancashire with its factories and railways. For most of Meredith's youth there were two pits – Black Park and Brynkinallt – operating behind the rolling hills that overlooked the village. Each pit had its own block of miners'

Countryside at Pontyblew, Chirk, where Meredith spent many happy childhood hours.

cottages set down in the green fields like incongruous chunks of some vast, distant city. Huddled in tight, serried rows, each separate community was connected with the next, and with the village in the valley below, by rough country lanes and well-worn pathways over gently sloping hills. Meredith remembered looking out of the back window of his home as a child in the early morning and seeing miners striding through the grassy fields, disappearing over the brow.

His grandparents had been country people. As part of the drift from a countryside in decline they had travelled into the Denbighshire area from Mid-Wales some seventy years previously in search of work. Billy's own father and mother had arrived in Chirk from Trevonin in the year of his birth. There is a story that he was born on the way, in a cart. Weak and puny and not expected to live, he is said to have been placed in a warm oven by his grandmother to keep him alive.

His father and elder brothers all worked at Black Park when he was a boy. The brothers soon moved on, but the father remained as an engine-winder until his death and Billy, on leaving school, joined him in the summer of 1886.

He was twelve years old when he began work in the mines. His first job was at the bottom, unhooking the tubs. Then he became a pony-driver. Afterwards he tackled 'hutching', pushing the tubs along the line where the ponies could not go. Later he began firing the boilers at the bottom of the pit, for it was his ambition to go in for engineering, like his father and brothers.

Meredith worked in the mines for eight years, from childhood through adolescence, and the experience continued to shape his attitudes and outlook for the rest of his life. In many ways he was lucky to be working and living where he was, not only because Chirk was such a beautiful spot (as a boy and youth he swam in the rivers, fished, and walked for miles) but because Black Park was a pit that always seemed to be in production, even when times were particularly bad for the industry as a whole.

There had been a coal mine at Chirk since 1653, making it one of the oldest in Wales. In 1877 a company of Lancashire men had bought it, and the manager-secretary, James Darlington, was by all accounts a fair-minded and popular man in the village. He had helped build the parish hall and the local cottage hospital and seemed genuinely concerned to ensure that the men at Black Park worked as regularly as possible and received as fair a wage as was possible. But for all his philanthropic concern, Black Park remained part of a wider, harsher industrial world, and during the 1890s there occurred two disastrous strikes that caused much suffering and strife in the industry.

In 1892, there was a national stoppage over a pay demand; with no national union, miners' organisations were rudimentary. The local Press reported, somewhat disdainfully, that 'gangs of strikers were parading in the Oswestry area' but the strike failed. However, in 1893 the Coal Owners' Association announced a twenty-five per cent cut in wages and this time the struggle was a longer one. Great efforts were made to bring all mining areas into a national federation, and a principal organiser and propagandist was George Rowley, of Black Park. By August 1893, soup kitchens were being set up in Wrexham. Relief organisations were distributing bread and potatoes to miners' wives – at Rhos, near Chirk, women fainted in the crush of people queuing to receive free food. The men received fourpence a day lockout money and though there was little violence, the divisions in local communities went deep. Chirk's second colliery, Brynkinallt, continued working throughout the dispute despite local protests and demonstrations. In November, Prime Minister Gladstone intervened and the men went back to work on their old rates of pay, to await the outcome of an enquiry that would look into the owners' attempts to cut wages. The strike was ultimately a failure; a year later Billy Meredith left the industry for good, but the struggles and the resulting hardships he had witnessed, and taken part in, left their mark on him. The lessons he had learnt he would take with him into his new profession of football.

In later years, when he was at the height of his fame as a footballer, much light-hearted fun was made of the fact that had his mother, on the night of his birth, travelled a few hundred yards further, then he would have been born an Englishman. Chirk stands, quite literally, on the border, but for Meredith the distance might have been a hundred

THE VIADUCT AND AQUEDUCT

The viaduct at Chirk.

miles; he was a fervent Welsh patriot and enjoyed proclaiming the fact, particularly when confronted with some example of English perfidy or arrogance.

He could not, however, speak Welsh and thus was deprived of a principal means of demonstrating his 'Welshness'. Indeed, for many men and women like Meredith, Wales was very much an idea – and an idea under threat. The industry of England, plus its roads and railways, had already penetrated deep into Wales, breaking down and engulfing traditional agricultural communities, hindering the growth of a separate Welsh nationality. Welsh culture was primarily agrarian; the industrial city and town were simply England writ large. The school which Meredith attended taught no specifically Welsh curricula, certainly not the language. The mines where he worked were owned and run by Englishmen (and thus the misery and hardship caused by the strikes were seen in Wales as being a direct consequence of English greed and intransigence).

However, no doubt as a reaction to these rapid and disturbing changes, a national consciousness was growing throughout the second half of the nineteenth century – the Eisteddfod movement began at this time and a religious revival had, by the 1890s, already left its mark on the hundreds of small industrial communities scattered up and down the Welsh valleys.

Meredith's family was typical in the latter respect. Mother and father were Primitive Methodists, regular chapel goers, the Bible being the only book in the house. Billy himself, though not as fervent a Christian, and certainly not a regular at chapel, could quote the Bible and enjoyed reading it. His eldest brother Elias took his religion with him when he left Chirk for Liverpool and became a Salvationist – the first man to wear the Salvation Army uniform in the streets of Wigan where he settled and later rose to the rank of sergeant-major. In later years, when visiting Billy's public house in Manchester, he would defiantly whistle hymns as he walked through the front door. Like the rest of the family, Billy included, he was teetotal. Brother Jim was well-known in Denbighshire as a lay preacher. He travelled to the Holy Land and returned to give lectures on his experiences there. Two of Billy's six sisters became nurses, one rising to become the matron of a cottage hospital. In both cases their religion had been their inspiration for following such careers.

9

Meredith's eldest brother Elias, engine driver and Salvationist. He took young Billy to see top professional teams. Meredith's sister Caroline delivered the infant Billy and later became Matron of Shrewsbury Cottage Hospital.

For Billy, however, the road to self-expression was always to be via football – in particular the Welsh international team. By pulling on the Welsh jersey he would demonstrate his affinity in a satisfyingly tangible way, could wage symbolic war against the English; the most bitter battles would always be against England. Playing for Wales would be, at times, almost a penance. For a perfectionist like Meredith, used to triumph and victory, the constant drubbings at the hands of the old enemy were frustrating and almost always fruitless. But he would never, it is certain, have swopped jerseys. Never, despite his occasional protestations at the bad luck of it all, and teasing references to those hundred yards to the border, would he have played for England. It seemed to suit his sentimental view of his country – 'Poor little Wales' as he was apt to say – and Wales would be his first, his dearest grievance. The necessity to leave Wales and travel to England would form a large part of that grievance.

Yet whatever Meredith did, wherever he went, Chirk would remain

Meredith's brother Jim, a lay preacher who visited the Holy Land. He later became a shop-keeper in Llangollen.

Brother Sam pointed the way by leaving Chirk to play professional football. He was Billy's best friend and a bachelor. Sam shared in Wales' great championship triumph of 1907, and music-hall star George Robey provided the team and publicity for his Benefit.

the emotional focal point of his life, where he could trace all his formative influences: his close-knit, clannish family, providing him with security, encouragement and example; his school, where he was fortunate enough to be taught by T.E. Thomas, the pioneering Welsh FA administrator and inspiration behind Chirk's remarkable contribution to Welsh international football; and last, but not least, the mines where he worked, which provided the bulk of players for the local Chirk team in which Meredith first found fame at the age of sixteen.

There are men still living in Chirk today who can recall how

Sam Meredith with his dog. After his playing days were over, Sam took a pub in Manchester.

important football was to them as miners. Each evening they would hurry from work to expend whatever energy they had left in the wind, mud and gathering darkness of the football pitch – 'Still in black-face, sometimes we'd rush up, no time for supper – our mothers and wives would complain – and out on to the field. Sometimes if we had a proper game we'd have a taxi and we'd change on the way.'

Romantic hindsight perhaps, but there was, before the turn of the century, little else by way of entertainment; all over industrial Britain, football had become an obsession. Meredith recalled, 'All my brothers were players. Elias, the eldest, was fond of football, but he didn't play as much as Jim, a right full-back, and Sam, a left full-back, who went on to play for Stoke.' Sam, in fact, pointed the way by leaving Chirk to become a professional player when Billy was still a boy.

Elias was instrumental in taking Billy to see top professional teams. An engine driver working for the Manchester and Yorkshire Railway Company, he could take Billy free of charge to watch Liverpool and Everton. In those early days, when the crowds were particularly large, he would hoist Billy on to his shoulders, and it was on just such a trip that Billy claims he saw the great Preston 'Invincibles' who won both Cup and League in 1889, the first team to do so. Billy was then fourteen and the performance of Jack Gordon, a winger with a dashing unorthodox style, made a great impression on him.

Closer to home, his village club had one of the most successful working-class amateur sides of their day and the mines where Billy worked provided the bulk of the players. The 1870s and 1880s were the heyday of North Wales soccer, a memorable boom time when crowds sometimes three deep lined the touchlines for Welsh Cup-ties. The Dee Valley was, as Peter Corrigan put it, 'a ten-mile stretch of country where soccer first found fertile ground in Wales' (*100 Years of Welsh Soccer*, Welsh Brewers Limited, 1976). Thousands watched Wrexham, Newton, Ruabon (home of the famous Druids club), Oswestry and Chirk. As industry in the area grew and thrived, so too did Association Football. By the turn of the century both had declined; the focus shifted south, where it has remained ever since.

Today, Chirk is a quiet country village again. Black Park closed in 1950 and Brynkinallt followed a few years later, while the football club no longer competes in top amateur football. Standing on the pitch watching local youngsters kicking a ball about, it is hard for the observer to imagine how Chirk could once have been such relative giants. But their record remains.

Between the years 1887 and 1894 they appeared in six Welsh Cup Finals, five times successfully. Meredith played in the last two, losing in 1893 but winning his first important medal in 1894 when Westminster Rovers were defeated 2-0.

He had made his debut in the first team, after a season or two in the reserves, in September 1892. Chirk first team was then competing in the Combination League, a semi-professional competition which included the reserve teams of large clubs like Everton and Stoke, plus smaller town teams like Macclesfield and Gorton Villa. The first mention of him playing occurs in October, in a match against Everton: 'The Welshmen then attacked and Meredith sent in a beauty'.

His tremendous shooting powers were a feature of many subsequent reports, and by late October, after a 10-1 defeat of Gorton Villa,

T.E. Thomas, Billy's schoolmaster and the champion of Welsh soccer.

the *Border Counties Advertiser* could say: 'Meredith, one of the home forwards, played a storming game for his side, and in him Chirk have one of the best forwards in the district.'

His career with Chirk was, however, an intermittent one. After one full season – 1892-3 – the climax of which was an appearance in the Welsh Cup Final at Oswestry against Wrexham, Meredith spent his second season as a senior dividing his time between Chirk, Northwich Victoria and even, on one occasion at least, Wrexham. This was 1893, a turbulent year. The miners' strike affected all aspects of local life, not least the organisation of football. Perhaps because of the difficulty of running the club during the strike – poor attendances, little money for travelling – Chirk dropped out of the Combination and concentrated on the Welsh League. A number of Chirk players immediately began playing for Wrexham who had remained in the Combination. Money was the main reason for the switch. Small though the amounts were, for men on strike it meant food and dignity. Meredith went a step further and accepted an offer from Northwich Victoria, then competing in the Second Division of the Football League. Northwich were able to pay expenses plus between five shillings (25p) and ten shillings (50p) a match. When the strike ended and life returned to normal in Chirk, Meredith reappeared in the Chirk team along with a number of the other 'mercenaries', and by the turn of the year the club had embarked upon a challenge for two Cups – the FA Amateur Cup, then in its first year of existence, and the Welsh Cup. Chirk reached the last four of both Cups but unfortunately the semi-final dates clashed. The FA ordered Chirk to play on the said date, which Chirk found impossible. They went on to victory in the Welsh Cup Final for the last time in their history.

Thus Meredith as a youth played against teams and men whose experience and skills were not far below First Division standards. Though drawing upon a population of just over a thousand, Chirk had competed with some success in the Combination before having to withdraw, and had been more than a match for the illustrious Old Brightonians, whom they had defeated in the FA Amateur Cup quarter-finals. But then, many of his team mates in the Chirk side had played for professional League sides, and gained caps for Wales. The Chirk sides for Meredith's two Cup Final appearances included no less than seven Welsh internationals plus five men who had played

William Owen, a great Welsh international star before Meredith joined him on the Chirk right wing.

First and Second Division football. One man in particular had special significance for Meredith and that was William Owen, the Chirk inside-right.

Known as the 'John L. Sullivan of inside forwards', Owen had already won twelve caps before Meredith joined him on the Chirk right wing. He had also played for Newton Heath (later Manchester United). There is no way of knowing exactly how good a player Owen was. Meredith recalled much later that he was, 'the sort of player who displayed that unselfishness that makes a player shine.' Yet the official report on Welsh players for 1891-2 says Owen was, 'a hard-working forward, can play in any position, very tricky, a selfish player. . .'

Reading between the lines it would seem that Owen was the perfect partner for Meredith, who would always need a tough, hard player beside him to win the ball and release it for Meredith to race away down the wing. The two certainly developed an understanding. In Owen's benefit match, against Ruabon and District in April 1894, the two put on an exhibition: 'Meredith and Owen were cheered for a neat bit of passing which totally nonplussed the home backs.'

The two played together in the Black Park Colliery five-a-side team

WELSH INTERNATIONAL PLAYERS, 1891.

Versus Scotland.

James Trainer—(Wrexham and Preston NorthEnd)—Prince of Goalkeepers, but made several mistakes, which lost the match.

David Jones—(Chirk and Bolton Wanderers)—a splendid Back—good tackler—safe kick, and fully sustained his reputation.

Seth Powell—(Summerhill and West Bromwich)—plays a cool game, and tackles well—justified his selection, also played a good game against England.

Humphrey Jones—(Bangor and Queens Park)—the best Centre-Half for years—uses judgment, and tackles fearlessly; also played against England.

Charles Parry—(Llansilin and Everton)—a good Half Back, but was out of condition, and also got injured : played a splendid game against England.

Arthur Lea—(Wrexham)—a good hard working player—called upon at the last moment, and played in wrong position—appeared nervous and outclassed; played a good game against Ireland as Left Half—has only one arm.

Joe. Davies—(Chirk)—good Outside Right—splendid shot—plays well with William Owen—rather selfish.

William Owen—(Chirk)—a hard working Forward—can play in any position--very tricky—rather selfish; he and Davies played against England and Ireland also, and quite justified their selection.

William Lewis—(Bangor)—a speedy Forward and very clever--does not use sufficient judgment; also played against England.

J. C. H. Bowdler—(Rhayader)—a very fast, tricky Forward—good shot at goal—rather light.

W. H. Turner—Wrexham) —a dashing Centre-Forward—passes well to his wings—fair shot at goal, but rash ; played a good game against England.

Part of the official Welsh FA assessment for 1891-2, including some of the men with whom Billy played at Chirk.

18

along with three other Welsh internationals – E. James, J. Williams and M. Roberts – winning numerous cups and medals at local sports days. Owen, with almost two decades of football experience, was very much the young man's mentor in those early days, even acting as intermediary between Billy and the various managers and scouts who began to appear regularly in the early 1890s.

There cannot be much doubt that Meredith's natural talents would have brought him to the notice of League clubs sooner or later, wheresoever and for whomsoever he might have been playing. He was from the very start of his career a prolific and spectacular goalscorer. And playing for Chirk among so many seasoned and successful players, his dreams of following a professional football career were always likely to be given the best possible chance. And yet it could have been a different story. Meredith, despite his love for the game – 'My heart was full of it,' he once told Jimmy Catton, editor of *Athletic News* – had doubts as to the morality of playing a game for a living, doubts implanted by his parents, by his mother in particular. In his memoirs, Meredith wrote about his parents' attitude: 'So far as my father was concerned, I had never known him bother himself about his boys playing football. He cared nothing about the game and though he never tried to prevent us playing, he certainly never encouraged our love for the game in any way.

'Though I became famous as a footballer and certainly something of a national hero in Wales, as a result of the numerous international games I took part in, I do not believe that my dad took the trouble to see me play in more than one game, and then he gave me the impression that he felt he had wasted his time. He certainly seemed bored to death and puzzled to know how men could earn good money for playing such a game. Still, for all that he never interfered with his boys and allowed them to play football when and where they liked.

'My mother, however, held entirely different views. Her objection to the game when we were young was that it ruined our footwear and added to the expense of the family, which as I have said, numbered ten all told. I was compelled to keep my football out of her sight . . .

'My mother's objection to football as I grew older became even stronger. She was quite eloquent when she gave her views to Mr Parlby and Mr Chapman of the Manchester City club.

'She told them, "It is all very well for you gentlemen to leave your big cities and come to our villages to steal our boys away. You offer good money I know, and I suppose it pays you to do so or you would not come. But a mother thinks of other things besides money. Our boys are happy and healthy, satisfied with their work and their innocent amusements. You gentlemen come and put all kinds of ideas into their heads. Tell them they can get more money for play than they can for hard but honest work ... if Billy takes my advice he will stick to his work and play football for his own amusement when his work is finished." '

Throughout his career Meredith would assert that footballers should have a 'proper' job – that the time between matches was only idled away, that training could never be a full-time occupation. Though having a rather romantic picture of his mother and her views on money and football, particularly when viewed in the light of her son's grim financial struggles later on in his career, there was a definite reluctance on his part to turn professional and leave the mines. His mother, however, was not the only factor working against such a move. Insecurity, the possible boredom of a life spent in the city – these too played their parts. Had a career in the coal-mining industry been more certain of success – in particular his hopes of becoming an engineer – he might well have continued as an amateur or as a semi-professional player, turning out for whoever he wished, for there were plenty of men in the district who did just that, getting the best of all worlds. He himself had spent the 1893-4 season dividing his time between Chirk, Northwich Victoria and Wrexham. But increasingly the game was becoming more of a business, and clubs were demanding more of the men they paid. To have remained an amateur would have required a profession to fall back upon – and amateurs playing at the top level were now almost exclusively of middle-class origins. Working men had to choose.

But there were men close to Meredith who could argue a powerful case for Billy taking the professional plunge, not least his own brother Sam, a full-back with Stoke City. Sam was something of a black sheep in the Meredith family. He had never married and had left home some years before Billy to play professionally. The two brothers, though totally different personalities, were always to remain close friends, and it was Sam who, in 1894, was one of the louder voices calling to Billy from across the border. Then there was Di Jones, a local man from Ruabon and a great admirer of the young Meredith. Jones was the first local man to play in an FA Cup Final, part of the Bolton Wanderers defence of Somerville, Sutcliffe and Jones. Jos Davies, a family friend of the Merediths, had gone to Manchester in 1890 to play for Ardwick and later played for Sheffield United, where he played alongside men like Ernest Needham, Harry Thickett and the massive legend of a goalkeeper, William Foulke. All three men pressed their respective managers to approach Meredith. It must have been a difficult time for the young man, torn as he was in so many different directions.

Northwich Victoria, who might have been expected to retain Meredith in the 1894-5 season, proved to be only a stepping-stone in his career. They were a spectacularly unsuccessful side, finishing bottom of Division Two in 1894, winning just three out of twenty-four matches. Meredith appeared in all three wins, plus two of the club's three draws, scoring a hat-trick in a 5-3 win over Newcastle United. In December 1893, when Northwich drew with Woolwich Arsenal, the *Northwich Chronicle* football correspondent enthused over the young Welshman's play: 'Meredith was fully on the alert and it wasn't long before the leather was passed over to him to deal with. This he did in a beautiful manner, getting past the backs and sending in a 'stinger' which Jeffries saved with much difficulty. The ball having been only sent a few yards out of goal, the forwards pushed to the front and Meredith again secured it and put in a beauty.'

Though capable of beating teams like Nantwich 12-0 in the Cheshire Cup (Meredith contributing a hat-trick including a penalty) Northwich Victoria were out of their depth and the following season they returned to the calmer waters of the Combination League where, as an amateur side once more, they continued to struggle. The same season, 1894-5, saw Meredith back permanently with Chirk in the Welsh League.

It was clear, however, that he had outgrown the parochial confines of Welsh football, indeed he seemed to be positively bursting out. Playing at centre-forward he scored eleven goals in three games at the start of the season, all five goals against Westminster Rovers in mid-March: 'A minute later Meredith accepted a pass from the right and after a splendid run in which he beat the half-back and backs, scored one of the prettiest goals seen for some time on the Chirk ground.'

21

In the same month Chirk travelled to Sheffield United for a friendly, where, despite the assistance of Sam Meredith at full-back, they were beaten 5-1. They also visited West Manchester and drew 1-1 with the Lancashire League side. Meredith was thus being seen on a wider stage and the expected offers seemed only a matter of time. However, it seemed that some managers were doubtful as to whether he could reproduce his dazzling ball skills regularly in the much tougher arena of First Division football: 'Di Jones of Bolton Wanderers came over to see me to persuade me to sign for his club. I should have been delighted to do so, for there I should have found more pals than I expected to find at Manchester . . . But Mr Bentley (the Bolton manager) had two objections to offer. First of all, I was too young; and secondly I was too light for his fancy.'

In November 1894, Ardwick of Manchester, lately re-named Manchester City, showed no such hesitation and signed him on amateur forms.

So little solid evidence remains of those distant days, no personal documents, precious few photographs, a few dubious, ghosted memoirs. Yet the departure of Billy Meredith seems to have touched Chirk people more deeply than that of a score of previous local men. Evidence for this is found in the many anecdotal stories once recounted concerning the signing of Meredith – each story retrospectively rueful, reflecting a sense of injured Welsh pride.

T.E. Thomas had led the campaign for the lifting of the ban on professionalism in Wales so that Welsh players might not be lured over the border in such numbers, but the football 'drain' was inevitable, given the relative wealth of individual towns and clubs in the industrial north and London. But though there was little future for professionals in Wales, there was still resentment – fuelled no doubt by the ever-growing Welsh 'consciousness'.

It was said that the two representatives from Manchester City were chased by local people and ducked in the village pond; that they had to disguise themselves; that they had to entertain Meredith's fellow miners in the local pub before they could be allowed to speak to him. Meredith himself, in his memoirs, tells a long, involved tale, complete with dialogue, the underlying message seeming to be that he was indifferent to and even scornful of the approaches.

'We don't like the idea of losing all our best players. Do you want to leave Wales, Billy?', a pal is supposed to have said.

'I don't and I'm not likely to, so you needn't worry,' was Meredith's reply.

Of course, such sentiments were hardly the point. Though Chirk had been successful in local football, they would remain a village team. To further his football ambitions meant having to join a bigger club. The delay in signing for Manchester City was due to Meredith's doubts about the nature of the professional game. There was, however, the possibility that a better offer might come from Bolton Wanderers or Stoke, perhaps. The City representatives persevered over the course of a long weekend and still Meredith would not sign professionally. Eventually, amid great secrecy, he signed as an amateur.

'I made known the terms I had to offer and neither Mr Chapman nor Mr Parlby could get me to budge an inch from them. I was prepared to sign a League form and play as an amateur for Manchester City. But I was to be allowed to remain at home and continue my work in the mine. I recognised that travelling backwards and forwards from Wales to Manchester each weekend was going to make football a much harder task for me. But the sacrifice of my home life would have been a far harder task and I absolutely refused to entertain the idea for a single moment.'

In later years Meredith was to claim that he regretted not holding out a little longer. Sheffield United, he discovered, had been about to offer him a £40 signing-on fee. Manchester City were eventually to pay him £5.

One of the oddities of Meredith's eventual choice of club was that, on the surface, City might have appeared no more enticing a prospect than Northwich Victoria. Meredith had played twice against Ardwick (City's previous name) during his Northwich season – thus it can be established that his first game at Hyde Road was in January 1894. The Manchester club had ended the season in dire financial straits, just two places above Northwich Victoria. But there the two clubs' destinies parted. During the close season, Ardwick had been reformed, floated themselves as a limited company and renamed Manchester City. They were an enthusiastic club but there were other reasons why Meredith might have chosen them.

The city of Manchester already had a long tradition of signing Welsh players. Both Ardwick and rivals Newton Heath had benefitted

The Hyde Road Hotel in Ardwick and the birthplace of the club which became Manchester City. The old Hyde Road ground was reached by going through the gates on the left. The pub renamed the City Gates, is now derelict.

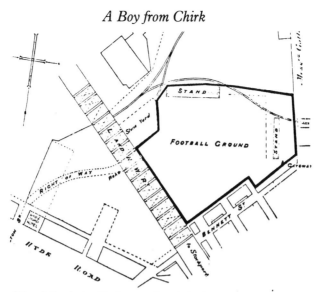

Plan of Manchester City's ground at Ardwick in 1894, showing the entrance from Chesters' Hyde Road Hotel

from the link. Indeed, Ardwick and Chirk had been playing friendlies ever since 1890. What is more, there were ex-Northwich players at City with whom Meredith had played, in particular Pat Finnerhan, a flamboyant, talented inside-right who was to take up the torch that William Owen had now relinquished. Finnerhan had been so impressed with the young man that he had urged the City board to approach Meredith in the summer of 1894.

There was also the fact that John Chapman, the City chairman and prominent in signing Meredith, was himself a Welshman, his family originating from the same Denbighshire region. Thus the Welsh links were strong.

Then there was the fact that City could hold out the prospect of a job in engineering, Meredith's first ambition. Galloway's, the world-famous boilerworks, were close by the City ground and had been one of the club's first patrons. There is some evidence to suggest that Meredith did work at Galloway's for a short time after joining the club. There were comfortable digs available for him in Clowes Street, a few hundred yards from the ground, where he could stay whenever he wished. Yet above all, it was the enthusiasm of the club and its servants that probably played the most important part in persuading him to sign.

Of the two men most closely involved in the signing, Joshua Parlby, the club secretary, would have been the more talkative. A larger than life character, he too has been swallowed up in myth and anecdote until it is hard to distinguish the hard facts of his life. But his jovial nature, his apparent zest for life, are attested to by all who knew and wrote of him. 'Falstaff' was the favourite epithet used to describe him; he was energetic and shrewd and, Meredith claims, it was Parlby's persuasive tongue that finally tipped the balance: 'There are some men whose silver tongues are said to have the power of charming song-birds from the trees, and I believe "Josh" Parlby was one of them.'

Within a week of his signing, Billy Meredith was on a train crossing England to Newcastle to play his first match for his new club.

For the next thirty years or so, Meredith would play football for one or other of the Manchester clubs. He would make his home in Manchester, live a long and eventful life there and be buried in the city's Southern Cemetery. During that time, Manchester would change out of all recognition. It was in the process of changing when he first arrived.

In 1894, the Manchester Ship Canal was opened by Queen Victoria, climaxing half a century's rapid development that had placed Manchester at the heart of Britain's industrial empire. Fifty years before, Ardwick Green – where Manchester City had its home – was as much countryside as Chirk Green. By the 1890s, however, the area was alive with industry of all kinds and the Hyde Road, cutting through it, was a dirty, dangerous major thoroughfare frequently jammed with horse-drawn traffic, characteristic of what Engels had called the 'girdle of squalor that ringed Manchester'.

The area was dominated by extensive railway sidings to the north. Clustered close to these vital supply lines were timber wharves and yards, claypits and potteries, ironworks and, serving these, numerous transportation firms – carriers and carriage-builders, waggoners and carters. Small factories and numerous small craftsmen abounded in the area, their shops and yards clustering along the Hyde Road. Back-to-back terracing had almost engulfed what open land was left, the lines of chimney-pots stretching from Ardwick Green, on the boundary of the original city of Manchester, all the way to Belle Vue – once the pleasure gardens for a more genteel population, but by 1894 a popular race-track and zoo.

City's Hyde Road ground was set in the very centre of this grimy

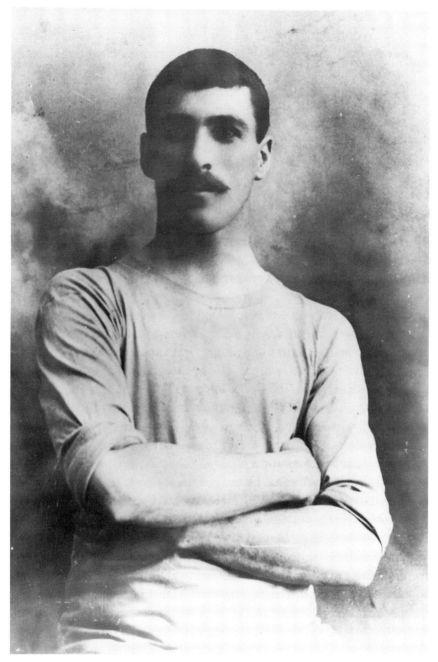

The young Meredith in the colours of Manchester City.

melee. A piece of apparently useless derelict ground in the shadow of the railway arches had been cleared and roped off with a colliery wire; a small stand had been erected. Overlooked on three sides by railway yards, engineering works and timber yards, hemmed in on the fourth by the terraced housing of Bennett Street, it was by no stretch of the imagination a picturesque setting.

The club had originally been a church organisation, like so many football clubs, linked to the nearby St Mark's Church in Clowes Street, the vicar serving as club chairman. But it had evolved away from its ecclesiastical roots and had been adopted by local working men to become a purely sporting organisation, a focus for a few men's athletic activities and a venue for the entertainment of many more.

The actual venue had shifted year by year, the team colours had changed almost with each move, even the name had been altered, added to, then dropped entirely. But by 1887, with the renting of the Hyde Road ground from a local brewer, the club had settled down into being something a little more ambitious.

The club's chief benefactor was Stephen Chester Thompson, managing director of Chester's Brewery, one of the biggest brewers in the city, controlling scores of public houses in Ardwick and Gorton. Chester Thompson was a local politician, agent for A.J. Balfour who was also persuaded to become a patron of the club. Thompson had lent the club money for a stand in which his own bars were granted a monopoly; he had paid for the club's very first professional. And thus, by some mysterious process, a mixture of motives part financial, part philanthropic, part social-athletic, the club had established an identity for itself and become its own reason for continuing to exist. In 1894, having failed financially because it had overreached itself and its patron, those in control launched the club as a limited company with shares of £1 each. A wide cross-section of the local population subscribed – working men as well as businessmen – and a newer, much grander name was suggested.

Today, as in Chirk, the traveller in search of tangible evidence of this particular past will find nothing: no terraced housing, no industry, no St Mark's Church, nor even Clowes Street. Only the railway arches remain and, a few hundred yards on, a large squat public house, once the Hyde Road Hotel and the City club's first headquarters. Empty now, the roof stripped, it is a derelict hulk awaiting demolition. Behind it, through the railway arches where spectators once hurried in their thousands, the original Hyde Road playing surface is now the skid-pan of a municipal bus depot.

Two weeks after signing for Manchester City, Meredith made his home debut at Hyde Road – changed in the pub and walked through the arches on to the ground to face local rivals Newton Heath. He scored two goals, his first for the club.

He wrote later: '. . . I got a little cheer to myself as I trotted off and I had the satisfaction of knowing that I had made a good start in my first home match.'

Merry Legs

2

'Merry Meredith'

'I had to travel to Manchester and then to Newcastle so that I did not make my debut under the best conditions. I was working in the pit on Friday and had to take the train at two o'clock in the morning. I was travelling until eleven o'clock, played the game and set off for home again, getting back at half-past ten on Sunday morning. The same night I had to go back to work in the mine so I had a somewhat strenuous weekend.'
Billy Meredith's memoirs, Topical Times, October 1919.

With a certain reluctance, Meredith eventually agreed to give up his full-time job at Black Park in the New Year of 1895 and sign professional forms. Though he had rooms in nearby Clowes Street, he continued to travel each week from Chirk to Manchester and back, occasionally turning out for the Chirk club in midweek. In his memoirs, he states that he continued working in the mine for four years after signing professionally for City, but this seems unlikely. In 1896, the club banned all their professionals from following any occupation other than football – an unpopular move at the time. Perhaps Meredith worked at Black Park during the close season; there is no way of knowing, because all the colliery records have either been destroyed or stolen, but it would have made sense. Meredith would have found it difficult to idle away his free time in such a strictly work-orientated household as his.

More significant perhaps, he was courting a local girl, Ellen Negus, through these early years and he was no doubt anxious to save what money he could. Whatever the reasons, Chirk was an infinitely more

Manchester City 1894-5, at the end of Meredith's first season with the club. Back row (l to r): Mr J.R. Prowse, R. Milarvie, D. Robson, C. Williams, F. Dyer, J. Broad (trainer). Middle: J. McBride, W. Bowman, T. Chapman, H. Clifford, G.E. Mann. Front: T. Little, J. Sharples, W. McReddie, A. Rowan, P. Finnerhan, W. Meredith.

attractive place than Manchester in which to spend his free time. Manchester was then a city at its drabbest and most workaday, with cobbled streets, darkly-dressed inhabitants, and ugly tramcars.

Moreover, the general ambience of the City club cannot have appealed to him, at least not in the beginning. City were a 'brewers' club through and through. The chairman, John Chapman, owned half a dozen public houses; Joshua Parlby was a publican; Chester Thompson was a brewer; there were even ex-players of the club like Bob Milarvie who had set themselves up as beer retailers on the Hyde Road. On top of all this, the club's headquarters was the Hyde Road Hotel, where the team often changed before the erection of proper dressing rooms. For one who had hardly ever tasted alcohol, let alone entered a public house, it must have been a distasteful business. Meredith was no prude, however. Being a very private man, not given to casual conversation, ill-at-ease amid public functions, he was happiest when walking by the local canal in the company of family and close friends.

'Ours was a happy family and to this day the memory of my youthful home life is sweet and fragrant,' he wrote in 1919. When the game was finished, he simply packed his bag and set off for home. The club seemed not to mind – Meredith was a reliable, dedicated player. In fact, in the four years or so that he was allegedly 'commuting' back and forth he only missed one game when his train was delayed by fog.

There is no doubt that he was an instant success on the field of play, however, and within a year of his debut the football correspondent of the *Athletic News* was to write: 'I don't suppose there is a man playing better football in the three Kingdoms. Nature has certainly endowed him with advantages above the common and, lithe of foot, an awkward customer to tackle, slippery as an eel, and a rare "buttocker" as they say in Cumberland, with shooting powers extraordinary, he is a real gem.'

Almost from the first there were doubts expressed in the Press as to how long he would stay at Manchester City. Bury, newly promoted neighbours, were said to have made an offer for him during the 1895-6 season and the popular newspapers were, as ever, keen to speculate. The *Athletic News* commented: 'Out of a quiet bit of spoof played on the City secretary on the night of the Newton Heath match . . . a great newspaper flutter has been made during the week. Out there came a startling paragraph to the effect that Bury had offered £150 for the transfer of the clever forward Meredith to Muffborough. Certainly the offer was made and by two worthies closely connected with the fortunes of the next biggest club to the Cottonopolis, but at the bottom there was no more idea of being serious than there was the probability of the City people listening to the voice of the 'charmer' yet . . . when an irresponsible Press bruited the rumour and 'drew' the Bury club to the extent of a disclaimer, the whole affair was suggestive of the First of April. As if a paltry £150 could tempt City, or as if £150 would tempt Meredith to think of going to Bury . . .'

Manchester City must have been well aware of the irony of the situation in which they found themselves. As Ardwick, the club had been censured by the FA on more than one occasion for 'poaching' players, illegally enticing them to break their contracts with other clubs. Yet a month after the new Manchester City club had begun its inaugural season, the first team had been severely disrupted by the activities of an American football agent who had illegally signed on four City players for a New York Soccer League. Hence the urgency with which Parlby and Chapman had hurried to Chirk to sign Meredith. Now Meredith himself was the target.

City were quite understandably prepared to pay him well, however, in order to keep him. Within a year he was earning £3 a week in winter, £2 a week in summer – good wages for someone of such limited experience. By 1900, he had doubled these figures and had already received a benefit (not a particularly successful one, as it turned out – he shared about £75 with goalkeeper Charlie Williams). Perhaps by the standards of some of the top English players his wages might have seemed less than sensational (in 1896, for instance, Tom Branden was receiving £7 a week all year round) yet there is every reason to believe that Manchester City were one of the most generous of clubs, where bonuses were concerned, outside of Division One. In fact, as we shall see, it was the directors' profligacy with money that was said to have caused much dissent among the team, with certain players, Meredith among them, often receiving more than the rest. In Meredith's case, the directors were wise to be generous.

While the possibility of an illegal approach could never be ruled out, the relatively free and easy days of the 1880s were ending and a club's hold over a player who had signed a contract was becoming tighter. The retain-and-transfer system, as it was called, was to irritate Meredith throughout his long career. It could well have been another reason for his apparent shyness in embracing the professional game. The power over his life that the directors had – even such good-natured and generous men as those who controlled Manchester City – angered him, particularly when he saw that he was being prevented from taking advantage of the good fortune he felt his natural skills deserved. This became more apparent to him when he stepped up on to the international stage and met players like Steve Bloomer and Charlie Athersmith, who were able to command extremely high wages.

It was not just a matter of money though. It was soon clear that Meredith was a complex character, quick to take offence, sometimes extremely moody, particularly when removed from his family circle. He needed a certain amount of 'jockeying along'. The loud, affable Josh Parlby was the perfect foil in this respect. In particular it appeared quite early on in his career that Meredith liked to get his own way on the field. In only his second season, at the age of twenty-one, he was appointed captain of City, an excuse to raise his wages above those of some of his older team mates, but also a sop to his vanity which was never inconsiderable. Though taciturn to the point

A youthful looking Meredith with Ellen Negus, his fiancee, soon to be his wife.

of silence in general conversation, he was not a modest young man where football was concerned and he took few people's advice. Though suggestions might be made to him as to how and where he should play, there was never any great expectation that he would listen.

Parlby once tried to switch Meredith to centre-forward to take advantage of his goal-scoring prowess. Joshua failed, as Meredith would have none of it. And City's first manager-secretary, Sam Ormerod, a phlegmatic, sanguine man, had only slight influence over the players. In an age when managers did not concern themselves with tactics, if such things could be said to exist then, Ormerod simply helped pick the team.

At first, however, Meredith was not the only important man in the team and was thus not allowed his 'head' completely. His inside partner for the first three seasons, Pat Finnerhan, with whom he had played at Northwich, was a great favourite with the Hyde Road crowd, and for a while seemed on the brink of an illustrious career. The 1895-6 season saw Manchester City challenging for promotion to Division One, with Meredith and Finnerhan leading the forward line in fine style. In November 1895, Finnerhan was selected to play for the Football League against the Irish League and scored a goal. The following April he was selected to play for the Professionals versus the Amateurs in an England international trial. Here he was playing alongside men like Billy Bassett, John Goodall, Ernest Crabtree, the giants of their day, and again Finnerhan scored.

But Manchester City failed to gain promotion and Finnerhan's career faltered. His form fell away and the England cap did not materialise. He was still popular in Manchester. The *Bolton Football Field* correspondent wrote: 'If dear old Pat is himself again, I expect to hear the "Welkins" (*the Sky Blues*) ring to his praises again.' But Finnerhan could not wait. He persuaded the directors to let him go to Liverpool in the First Division. He failed to establish himself in the first team and moved down to Bristol City in the Southern League. Eventually, in the same year that Manchester City finally reached the First Division, he returned to his native Northwich. Easy going and extremely likeable, Finnerhan could now concentrate on his other great love – possibly his greatest love if we are to believe J.J. Bentley who had tried to sign him for Bolton Wanderers – that of racing pigeons. In retirement Meredith and Finnerhan would sit in the old Drill Field stand and talk over old times, reminiscing, recalling the days when Meredith had to run across a plank at the corner of the ground to take corners, or when the crowd would jeer at Meredith, thinking him too frail, while cheering Finnerhan, the 'Greens' local hero.

With Finnerhan gone however, Meredith stood alone as the City club's principal asset, City's inspiration and their star. He was also to become the club's most consistent player, in that he was hardly ever injured despite being the obvious target for defenders. During his first five years at the club he missed only seven League games, three of those because he was playing for Wales and one because he was held up in fog. Despite being a right-winger, he scored goals with monotonous regularity. In those same first five seasons he was to be top scorer three times, scoring eighty-nine goals in 170 games, well over a quarter of all goals scored by the club. For a winger, these are impressive figures.

Quite soon, the names Manchester City and Billy Meredith were spoken of in the same breath; with the club's supporters he could do no wrong. He was a crowd-pleaser; with his speed, his powerful long-range shooting which produced spectacular goals and his baffling ball control that bemused many a heavily-built full back, he was perfectly equipped to give the people what they wanted, what all football fans have ever wanted – entertainment.

City drew large noisy crowds from the very first season, regularly pushing their way beneath the railway arches in the mud and packing the rough and ready grandstand, or swarming over the rudimentary terraces. Musical instruments such as bugles and drums would sound as City attacked, and on big occasions, even fancy dress would be worn. To read some of the match reports of the time, it would seem a festival-like atmosphere regularly prevailed amid the incongruous surroundings. And Billy Meredith played to this ill-assorted gallery, with body-swerves and backheels at speed, dipping shots from thirty yards – he was all dash and daring and already nicknamed 'Merry Meredith'.

But there was another side to the coin. Inevitably, as with all gifted ball-players, he had a tendency to overdo things. Ever since his days with W. Owen and Chirk, the charge of selfishness had occasionally been levelled. When playing with Pat Finnerhan, this trait caused concern: 'Meredith and Finnerhan almost exercised a monopoly of the ball for City and such a thing as a long pass seemingly does not come within their football knowledge ... good man as Finnerhan is, he only seems to have eyes for Meredith, and Meredith evidently thinks that when he gets the ball there is only one player on the field and that is himself. ...'

There might have been some excuse for such exclusivity during the early years. Sam Ormerod used over fifty players in just three seasons and with so many new faces coming and going, teamwork must have been difficult. But two years after Finnerhan's departure the problem remained: 'People have watched faithfully for captain Meredith to forget himself a little more and, having done his share with his usual brilliance, to remember the other forwards so often waiting to shoot from better positions ...', said the *Bolton Football Field*.

But such criticism only demonstrated how swiftly he had become the focus of attention and how expectations were always going to be

Puzzled Half Back: Well, I'm blessed! He can play backwards better than most chaps can play forwards.

high: 'He's set his own standards and we naturally look for its regular appearance. So far this season, Meredith's shooting powers have been far less accurate and his centres less dangerous than he has led us to expect from him. He has still the same hold on the crowd and the confidence in him and encouraging shouts bubble simultaneously with his possession of the ball. But, alas, the disappointed "Oh's!" are still too often to be heard.'

In Billy Meredith, Sam Ormerod and his directors had a wonderful asset that brought with it a tricky problem, that of how to balance the team and, in particular, the forward line. During those eventful first five seasons in the Second Division, City's left-winger was changed on no less than forty-five occasions with more than thirteen different players being used. As the majority of attacks in the 1890s developed down the wings, it was obvious that the ball would be sent out to Meredith rather than to an untried youngster with neither the authority to command the ball nor the unassuageable appetite for it that Meredith possessed. And with Finnerhan no longer present to shoulder some of the responsibility, each game tended to turn on how well Meredith would play or how effective the opposition were in stopping him.

There was a great deal of talk in the club programme of the directors' intentions to buy 'quality' players to complement him but, somehow, although a great amount of money was taken at the turnstiles, the expected transfers did not take place. Instead the management were inclined to buy older, more established and experienced men – 'proven players' as they put it at the time – but all too often these proven men were past their playing peak.

It is easy to see, and to understand, why such miscalculations were made. The City management were inexperienced in the arts of bringing on a successful football team. Times were changing. The 1890s saw football players' wages rising because the game as a commercial operation was expanding dramatically. With more and more money being invested, with publicity and prestige being translated into financial profits, the pressure for success was intensifying. The casual approach of the 1880s was being replaced by a more professional attitude at all levels of the game. Manchester City itself was to prohibit its professionals from working at any job other than football from 1896 on; the players were regularly taken away for 'special training' weekends to keep them from the debilitating temptations of the city, as much as to get them fit. Therefore, any shortcomings the directors might have regarding the management and motivation of their men were increasingly exposed.

At the end of the 1895-6 season City were the Second Division runners-up, and thus eligible for the Test matches which determined who went up to the First Division. The team played so badly and failed so ignominiously (with defeats of 8-0 and 6-1) that it could not be explained away in terms of football skill alone. Dissension among the players had been detected earlier in the season by a football correspondent. Its cause – money.

The *Athletic News* said: 'The gate at Hyde Road amounted to £789 and what with those who slipped the gatekeeper and those left outside, the City lost quite another £50. This beats the best of £697 when the Rovers were here. I think that it is this flushness of money that tempts the City directorate to be so prodigal in the way of bonuses to players and one thing and another. They have never yet had to exercise that talent in the way of making both ends meet. I rather think they might detach themselves from a lot of presumed responsibility and leave more in the hands of the secretary who has had too long an innings with first class footballers to know what is best.'

City team of the late 1890s with Chapman and Ormerod posing proudly with the side they built. Back row (l to r): Jimmy Broad (trainer), John Chapman, Bert Read, Charlie Williams, 'Buxton' Smith, William 'Doc' Holmes, Dick Ray, Sam Ormerod. Front: Billy Meredith, J. Whiteside, Billy Gillespie, 'Stockport' Smith. On ground: R. Moffat, F. Williams.

The 'little jealousies' hinted at led to some dubious behaviour on the field. It was even rumoured that bribes had been accepted, though this was never proved. Meredith himself thought that the problem lay with newer players being unsure as to whether they would be offered contracts if the club gained promotion.

Whatever the cause, once promotion had been missed, a number of players were sold, including three of Meredith's Welsh international colleagues – Chapman, Morris and Davies. The same correspondent commented: 'The only reason I can fathom for the supposed spring-clearance is that the management cannot handle them, which is tantamount to an acknowledgement of weak-kneed policy in the board room.'

The problem of money – payments to players etc – and its mishandling was not to disappear. In fact it was to bedevil Manchester City for a decade and almost cause the club's demise.

Meredith, needless to say, was bitterly disappointed at the failure to gain promotion and he, too, blamed the management. But gradually

Ormerod and Chapman, plus trainer Jimmy Broad, assembled a group of players very much, one suspects, in Ormerod's own image – solid, hard-working, unremarkable men capable of playing above themselves when inspired by their young captain. Even their names have a solid, dependable ring to them: Bert Read, a local man at right-back; Dick Ray, a left-back from Macclesfield; William 'Doc' Holmes, a centre-half from Matlock; plus two William Smiths – 'Buxton' at right-half and 'Stockport' at inside-right and Meredith's dependable partner. Another local boy, Fred Williams, was at inside-left, and two Scotsmen – Dougal and Cowie – managed to establish some continuity on the left wing.

Most important of all perhaps was the signing, in January 1897, of William Gillespie from Lincoln. Gillespie became Meredith's first truly dependable 'target'. He was large and strong and suited Meredith's style of play. A season after Gillespie arrived Wigan County came to Hyde Road for an FA Cup tie. On the right wing for County that day was the veteran Jack Gordon, once of Preston North End and Meredith's childhood hero. Gordon, it was noted by *Bolton Football Field*'s City correspondent, specialised in sending in low, fast centres, very much according to the textbooks of the day. Meredith, however, 'occasionally obliges in the same way but oftener than not makes a lofty centre which affords far less chance of scoring unless the front rank are of the 'kick and rush' order. Gillespie's cranium makes them especially treacherous.'

Goalkeepers, it must be remembered, could expect to be shoulder-charged if they held on to the ball, and Gillespie must have been a fearsome sight, charging in. J.C. Clegg, writing in the *Manchester Football News* in 1930, remembered: 'The way he would dive in to head the ball at the risk of maiming himself was enough to make the spectators shudder. At times he would literally hurl himself at the ball and not infrequently did he follow it into the net'.

Over the years Gillespie received his fair share of barracking from the 'popular' stand. A wholehearted player, he missed as many chances as he converted, but Meredith considered him 'one of the best centre-forwards I ever saw. He never flinched, was always up, kept his head, could take a centre and could get a goal on his own. It was a good job he laughed at his critics. He always had our confidence'.

In all, Gillespie was to spend almost nine years at Hyde Road scoring 120 goals in 217 games. He was a vital man in Meredith's early career and Meredith proved a valuable friend to the young Scot. The temptations of city life, referred to earlier, often proved too much for Gillespie. Drink, so plentiful at the City club, was a regular problem for him and he was dropped many times for failing to keep himself sober for games (though tales that he would often turn out drunk must be discounted). In fact, at one point, his career was in serious jeopardy. Meredith, though only a year or two older, took Gillespie in hand. They roomed together on special training weekends; Meredith organised fishing weekends (both men were keen anglers); he even held Gillespie's money for him, insisting that he bank a certain amount per week, and doling the rest out to him as and when he needed it. Elder brother Elias would have been proud of him.

From 1 October 1898, Manchester City were unbeaten in thirteen games and were certain of the Second Division title almost a month before the season's end. Theirs was an uncomplicated, direct method: with a solid, strongly-built defence behind them, the forwards charged ahead to bombard the opposing goal with shots from all angles. In February, they beat Darwen 10-0.

'After such a victorious issue you would expect to hear of clock-work movements from wing-to-wing and all the rest of the Aston-cum-Stokey-Villa class jargon. Such was far from being the case. Gillespie's, Dougal's and Meredith's goals were superb individual efforts – 'aid' in each of which would have been a misfortune,' said the *Athletic News*.

Gillespie was the battering ram: 'His tendency to push the goal-keeper through with the ball was in evidence throughout the game and often he missed the mark and had to find his way out of the network.'

In the last month of the promotion season, Meredith was joined on the right wing by a famous campaigner, Jimmy Ross, purchased from Burnley for £50. For Meredith, Ross's arrival was a personal thrill.

'I must confess that Ross will always be my favourite hero. He was good at everything he put his hand to and what he didn't know about football wasn't worth knowing. At billiards and card games he was an expert. Though he must have been thirty-four at least when he joined us, he was able to win seventy yards handicaps with ease and did so. He could talk like a lawyer and on and off the pitch his comic sayings had us in stitches.'

ROSS GETS A FACER

MEREDITH AND HIS QUILL

Athletic News, 16 October 1899.

Meredith's own apocryphal story of their first tactical talk reveals the respect he had for the little Scotsman. Until then no one had been able to dictate to Meredith what to do. Yet, as their first game together was about to start, Meredith took Ross aside and said, 'Tell me where you want me to stand and what you want me to do.'

'Oh, that's easily fixed up. You do the running, laddie, and I'll do the feeding and between the two of us we'll manage very well,' replied Ross.

Ross was a fiery character with an abrasive tongue and wit and an unscrupulous attitude to his job, having been brought up in the hard days of the 1880s. He had been at the centre of many a controversy. As far back as 1887, he had been mobbed by Queen's Park players after fouling one of their number. He had been a member of the famous Preston North End 'Invincibles' when his right wing partner had been Jack Gordon. He was already something of a legend, having scored eight when Preston beat Hyde 26-0 in the FA Cup. His brother was the famous Nick Ross, who on his death-bed had tried to get Jimmy to promise he would never leave Preston. But Jimmy moved on and had guided first Liverpool, then Burnley to promotion. Now he was to accompany Manchester City and Meredith, the new Jack Gordon, into the First Division.

In April 1899, Manchester City collected the Second Division trophy. There was talk of the club moving down the Hyde Road to Belle Vue where crowds of 40-50,000 could be accommodated; star names were going to be bought; at the very least a new covered stand would be built – a Grand Stand Company had been formed and a stand from the Fulham Pageant was bought and transported to Manchester. As the players dispersed for their summer break, the builders moved in. The future looked bright for Billy Meredith.

MANCHESTER CITY ASSOCIATION FOOTBALL TEAM.   SECOND LEAGUE CHAMPIONS.

City's Second Division championship-winning team of 1898. Meredith (extreme left of front row) was City's leading scorer with 29 League goals. Jimmy Ross stands behind him. 'Stockport' Smith sits to Meredith's left.

3

Rise and Fall

'Incident number two gave me the next goal also. A free-kick had been given against us and I was quite near my own goal when I fastened on to the ball. Carrying it at my toes I galloped down the field, the whole of the Derby team hot upon my heels. Keeping the lead the whole length of the field, I found myself with only Fryer to beat. Giving a mighty kick, I let fly at the goal and the keeper only just managed to touch the ball before it curled itself into the corner of the net, the force sufficient to send Fryer spinning. I rather liked that goal, thinking it above the average, and I can remember the chase I led the field that day.'
Billy Meredith's memoirs, Topical Times, October 1919.

Twenty-two thousand people, among them the Mayor of Manchester and A.J. Balfour, were packed into a refurbished Hyde Road ground to watch Meredith score that goal and a second from a curling shot-cum-centre from the corner-flag. Derby County were the opponents and City won 4-0. A week earlier, City had begun their career in the First Division at Blackburn, losing 4-3, when Meredith had scored Manchester City's first goal in the First Division.

The Derby match, however, seemed to have been the moment all Manchester's sporting public had been waiting for – Meredith and City in the First Division at last: '. . . as for Meredith, Bloomer may well pass the remark that there isn't a finer right-wing in the Kingdom. William was master of the situation from start to finish: tricking, combining, dribbling, blocking superbly. Fresh as a daisy throughout, signalling to his custodian to send him the ball at the

45

MERRYLEGS

very finish. A fine testimonial to the careful manner in which he looks after himself. Trainer Broad skipped about like a schoolboy when the captain showed his pursuers a clean pair of heels and finished with a screaming shot, but the screw into goal from which Meredith converted a second point was perhaps a better masterpiece. . .' (*Bolton Football Field*).

'For real brilliance the right-wing took the biscuit. Meredith is quite as good in superior company as when opposed by second-class men. In fact, there are few, if any, better men at outside-right. His partner, the veteran Ross, of whom it is predicted every season that he has had his day, is in reality taking a second lease of footballing life, despite the paucity of head-covering, and as a wing the two will cause some trouble.' (*Athletic News*).

Meredith's claiming of the match ball was very much in character. He collected mementoes of all kinds, tangible symbols of victory and defeat – proof, as it were, of his achievements and his ever-growing

Cope was unable to cope with Meredith last Saturday.

stature in the game. He began, during this period, to collect newspaper cuttings of his career, sticking them into large scrapbooks that he would keep all his life. He was also keen on the statistics of his playing days and kept notes on goals he had scored, games he had played, notes that in later years would prove as notoriously unreliable as his rather selective memory. He had, for instance, a tendency to credit himself with goals that others had actually put into the net. In his memoirs he wrote of his debut match in the First Division: 'From the corner flag I kicked at goal and the ball curled under the bar but, striking the upright bounced back. To save disputes Gillespie promptly headed it into the net but it was agreed that I had scored the goal all right, and at that time I was supposed to have taken out a patent for goals of this kind.' One senses he would have been most sympathetic to the American system of crediting 'assists'.

Then again, he would sometimes include in his total of games played matches he had, in fact, missed while playing for Wales. He was not being devious – he simply felt that because he had been selected and would have played anyway, then the games should be included. Such behavioural quirks and eccentricities were to become more pronounced in his old age. By then he had perfected a repertoire of 'odd' responses, cantankerous leg-pulling, a conscious 'hamming' in order to irritate and provoke. As a young man there was little need, little opportunity, to shock and puzzle gullible journalists. As Manchester City entered the First Division, Meredith was in his prime as a footballer – twenty-six years old, his apprenticeship served in the Second Division, his method and style of play perfected. Nevertheless, as his public stock rose, so too did the occasions upon which he felt himself unfairly, unjustly thwarted. Indeed, his first spell in the First Division could be said to have been one of the most frustrating, unsatisfying he was ever to experience.

Outwardly, however, life seemed to be about as perfect as it could be for Billy Meredith. In 1901, he finally married his childhood sweetheart from Chirk, Ellen Negus, at St. Mark's Church in Clowes Street.

Last Saturday, Meredith was bubbling over with trickiness
– to Cowell's dismay.

At a dinner given some days later to celebrate Manchester City's victory in the Manchester Cup, the directors presented Meredith with a gold watch and his wife with a silver-mounted satchel and a gold bracelet. For the mantelpiece of their new home, the players presented the couple with a marble clock.

The Merediths moved into a house provided by the club in Nut Street, backing on to Belle Vue, a mile or so from the City ground. A two-up, two-down terraced dwelling that remains standing today, it presented a trim and tidy image that was to epitomise Meredith's football life. His was to be, for the next twenty years, a routine existence dedicated to football. His wife ran the home and eventually produced two daughters. She took little interest in football and hardly ever attended a game, which suited her husband who felt that football grounds were not fit places for women anyway. Though she enjoyed the social life that football occasionally afforded, Meredith did not.

They lived a comfortable existence, even a privileged existence for working people at the turn of the century. By now he was earning £6

Meredith's marriage to Ellen Negus. Apart from his brother Sam, on the far right, the guests pictured are all from the Negus family.

Meredith's first home in Nut Street, as it is today.

a week, winter and summer, more than double what a skilled worker in industry might earn and well beyond his former colleagues back at Chirk's Black Park Colliery. Thus, the Meredith family ate well, were able to afford fine furniture and luxuries such as a piano. Their girls were able to take private dancing lessons. The family spent each summer in Chirk, of course, and their eldest daughter even went to school there for part of the year.

Their standard of living was of more importance to Ellen than to Billy. He lived an almost spartan existence, virtually unchanged in its unvarying routine from his single days in digs at Clowes Street. His life revolved around the professional footballer's cycle of playing and preparing to play. He had special diets to which he rigidly adhered, particularly the match-day routine of a glass of port before the game and a boiled chicken afterwards. The Meredith household on that most important of days was geared entirely to his needs. He spoke little, was inclined to be short-tempered and sullen. Ellen Meredith would hurry about keeping her two girls quiet and out of the way until at last she would open the door for him to pass through, handing him his bag with his kit inside – a leather bag with his initials WM embossed in gold on the side. Temperamentally she complemented him in much the same way as Josh Parlby had done in the early days. Her family had come originally from Yorkshire and she was outspoken, talkative and lively; she would be able to humour him, take no nonsense, goad him on and yet appear to let him have his own way. He would always remain a private man – self-sufficient and even self-obsessed, especially where his own physical condition was concerned.

His apparent immunity from injury and the fact that he missed only a handful of games throughout his thirty-odd years as a professional was once a legend and a source of great pride to him. Today's professional footballers might point to the fact that Meredith had far fewer games to get through in a season and thus was unlikely to suffer from the modern stress-induced injuries – ligaments, hamstrings, groin and pelvic strains etc. Yet Meredith stood out even in his own day when injuries were of the sort one would expect from a more physical game – broken arms and legs, collar-bones and other 'contact' injuries.

Part of the answer must lie in his extraordinary balance, his natural agility and the speed with which he was able to avoid many of the more clumsy challenges. He was naturally tough and wiry – he would always claim, tongue in cheek, that working in the mines from the age of twelve had toughened him up and that leaping out of the way of runaway coal trucks had sharpened his wits.

But he certainly spent considerable time looking after himself physically. He was also knowledgeable where massage was concerned. Two of his sisters were nurses and his wife Ellen had also trained for nursing. He could also draw upon his grandmother's knowledge of herbal remedies, comfrey being a particular favourite of his for healing strains and sore muscles. He used various lotions to keep his muscles supple. His daughter Winnie remembers a foul-smelling ointment he called 'dog fat' – sometimes used on mining machinery – that he would smear over his legs and torso. Certain secret embrocations he later patented and sold in the sports shop he was to have in St. Peter's Square. Meredith was also a devotee of John Allison, a club

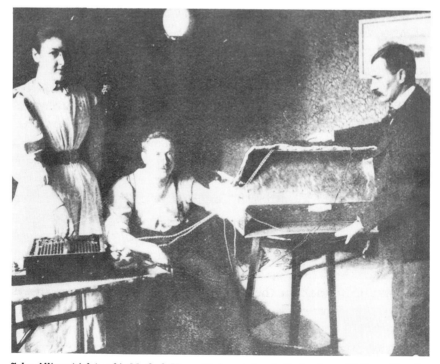

John Allison (right) at his Matlock House Hydro, giving the Stoke player, Mellor, a 'dowsing radiant heat bath' for an injured arm

director, the proprietor for many years of the Matlock House Hydro on the Hyde Road, almost opposite the City ground. This establishment specialised in revolutionary heat treatments of sporting injuries, treating football players, in particular, from all over the country. Meredith might have looked askance at the 'modern' methods, but certainly benefitted from Allison's knowledge.

In many ways, Meredith was ahead of his time in the care he lavished on the treatment of even minor injuries in an age when medical care for working people was rudimentary, and the awareness of footballers concerning their physical fitness and the treatment of their particular injuries was almost primitive.

A perfect example of the ignorance prevalent at the time was the sad death of Di Jones, the famous Welsh full-back, Bolton FA Cup Finalist, the man who tried to get Meredith to join the Trotters. He had joined Manchester City at the start of their promotion year, had taken over the captaincy from Meredith at a crucial time in the club's history. In August 1902, during a pre-season friendly, Jones had fallen and gashed his knee quite badly. He had been treated by the club's doctor and had gone home to convalesce. Within a week he was dead – the wound turned septic because it had not been properly attended to and because Jones had not taken it seriously enough.

By contrast, Meredith treated his body as seriously as any modern athlete might; his Methodist chapel upbringing had resulted in his being teetotal – certainly not the case with many of his team mates – and he did not smoke. One almost senses that he felt obliged to be as professional as he could – that anything less than complete dedication to his task was morally wrong. He was prevented from following any other occupation while he played, and so football was his trade. Even before his marriage he had wasted little of his spare time, and when official training was over he would return to the ground and practise ball-control, centring and corner-kicks, over and over again. Living in Nut Street he could step out of his back garden and on to the Belle Vue track, then back for the inevitable bath. The house was always full of steam, Winnie his daughter recalled, when her father was at home.

This regular, almost humdrum, existence was in sharp contrast to the life he led in the increasingly popular world of professional football. He was becoming something of a celebrity, a character whom thousands recognised, imitated, wondered at. Cartoonists were beginning to depict him, bandy-legged, moustached and, from the very start, with a quill, or toothpick, jutting out from between his lips. It was Meredith's gimmick – his trademark – and he appreciated its value.

'It's wonderful what trifles make a man famous. Long after my fame as an internationalist has become dead, my name will be remembered as the man who required a toothpick to help him play football. Hundreds of people have asked me if my toothpick is my mascot. I reply with truth that it isn't. And yet I confess that I would probably be put off my game if I found myself forced to part with my old pal. And I am sure many cartoonists would miss the bit of wood as much as I should. For it must be admitted that in some cases I should not have recognised myself if the artists hadn't been more successful in drawing the toothpick than its owner.'

How he came to acquire the toothpick, he explained, was simple. As a miner he had chewed tobacco. When playing he had continued to chew and sweat and spit the juice – a messy habit. But he needed to chew something and eventually hit upon a toothpick after a meal, and thus the toothpick had arrived. It was later to become a minor craze. Admirers would send him toothpicks just as pop fans would later send jelly babies to pop stars.

As he shrewdly acknowledged, cartoonists seized on the gimmick and, in the very first cartoon depicting him (fittingly he is accompanied by Jimmy Ross), the toothpick is prominent.

There is no doubting the fact that he enjoyed his new-found fame, particularly as, by 1900, it had spread back to Wales. In the Principality he was fast approaching the legendary status normally accorded then, as now, only to rugby players. For almost five years he had been selected regularly for Wales and was regarded as a national hero – a player on a par with any Englishman.

He had made his debut in 1895, against Ireland in Belfast. After a turbulent trip across the Irish Sea, during which Meredith had been extremely ill, Wales put on a good display and drew 2-2. Two days later, in London, Meredith had lined up for his first game against England – an experience he claimed that he would never forget. He had, he said, never before seen so many top hats in his life.

'The size of the ground was an eye-opener to us and the size of the

Billy Meredith poses wearing a Welsh international cap, one of the first he was to win.

team we had to meet also made us stare a little. Fine fellows they were, some six feet three in their socks and carrying plenty of weight with their inches. And they were not afraid to use their weight either, as some of us discovered. All in a true sporting fashion, of course, for they were just as ready to take as to give hard knocks. Every man of them could run like a deer and before the game was over most of us were crying bellows to mend. Most of them were Corinthian stars and they played the Corinthian game. 'Twas a grand sight to see their forward line sweeping down the field, though probably our backs didn't think so. . .'

It was the last time that an England team would consist entirely of amateurs and Wales held them to a draw. Men like Wreford-Brown, G.O. Smith and R.R. Sandilands were the cream of the amateur game, soon to be superseded by professionals.

Picked for the third match in the international season, to be played a week later in Scotland, to his dismay Meredith found that he was required by his club to play in a League match. They had the power to compel him – the Welsh FA could do nothing. He was not amused. 'When I went on the field that day I was suffering from a feeling of injustice having been done to me by my club. I was but a young player, to whom the honour of gaining international caps was very sweet and, like all Welshmen, my patriotism in those days was very pronounced ... however, the moment I step upon a football field I have no thoughts for anything but the game and Lincoln and not Manchester City had good reason to complain of the result of my Welsh blood being aroused that day, for I scored five goals.'

Thus began a struggle that was to continue until he was well into his maturity as a footballer – to be free to play for his country whenever his country wanted him. The money, he insisted, was unimportant – £1 a match. It was the principle – yet another aspect of the strange legal position of the professional footballer that was to cause him so much heartache. During the period 1895-1900 he was selected to play for Wales on eighteen occasions but he was forced to miss six of those games. Almost always it was the Scottish game he missed because that was played on a Saturday.

As a team Wales were not strong, even before being disrupted by forced withdrawals such as Meredith's. They had to draw upon a much smaller pool of players, of course, but what they lacked in breadth they gained in depth – of experience and acquaintance. The national team remained for decades a rather parochial affair – North Wales and Chirk in particular. In fact the Welsh selectors met at the Hand Hotel, Chirk, in 1892. Meredith's inside partners, for instance, were usually men he knew well – Jos Davies, of Chirk and Manchester City, and Parry from Wrexham, plus Vaughan and Butler of the Druids. The team managed to hold their own against the Irish, and the games between the smaller nations were usually quite pleasant affairs – Meredith always expressed an affinity with the Irish. But against the English everything was on a different scale.

The result of the 1895 match was proved the following season to have been unrepresentative – Steve Bloomer led a professional English team to a 9-1 victory, the great Derby man scoring five goals. In the next five seasons Wales scraped only one goal against the

The Welsh team before an international at Wrexham in 1901. Meredith is the player with the ball. The goalkeeper is Roose and the two players on the extreme right of the back row are Charlie Morris (Chirk and Derby) and Maurice Parry (Liverpool).

English, scant reward for all the physical and nervous energy the Welsh poured into the crucial encounter against England. But by 1900, with the Welsh FA taking the bold step of staging the game in the south, at Cardiff Arms Park of all places, there was a definite air of expectation. Meredith's name had come to mean something to the Welsh, both north and south, and his first appearance in the south had been eagerly looked forward to. 'The finest right-winger living,' the *Western Mail* had called him.

Within three minutes Wales, playing in white and green halved shirts – no fiery red jerseys in those days – were a goal down and it was the genius of Meredith that brought them back into the game. The winger had already tested England's goalkeeper with a shot from the touchline in the first half. In the second, Morgan Owen sent Meredith away with a magnificent long pass. Meredith rounded Oakley with ease before closing on Robinson and unleashing an unstoppable shot. Only the woodwork might have saved England but the ball crashed against the underside of the crossbar and then spun over the line and into the net. Welsh cheers deafened the players who came to congratulate the scorer. There were no more goals, Wales had held England, and the fans poured out into the streets of Cardiff, grateful at having seen Meredith, the boy from Chirk who had grown up into a Welsh legend.

Whether he was the greatest right-winger living would continue to be a keenly debated point in pubs and on the terraces. Now he was at last in the First Division, however, some sort of meaningful comparison could be made.

The current England winger was Charlie Athersmith of Aston Villa, and when the latter came to City to play an FA Cup match, the *Bolton Football Field* correspondent summed up the two men's contrasting abilities thus: 'Athersmith is not a great player in the true sense of the word. His method is to be as near offside as possible – sometimes in an out-and-out offside position. Therefore, he uses his speed to make sudden breaks and cause confusion. But for dribbling past half-backs and full-backs, Athersmith ranks a long way behind Meredith.'

All of which only underlined the apparent incongruity of Meredith remaining with Manchester City. With each close season came the same rumours, the same denials. Twice it had been reported that Tottenham Hotspur, who were spending a great deal of money trying to establish themselves as a force in the land, had secured Meredith's signature. The official Manchester programme for 3 September 1898 said: 'City ran a close shave of having to lose him when the close season set in. A southern emissary, formerly of the north, who now combines Cockney cheek with a northern assurance, nearly enticed him away. That individual will have a mixed reception when he appears again in Manchester. Meredith's re-signing meant an advance in wages. Fifty golding, glittering, soverings as the Cockney would say, thrown before a man are a great temptation. No wonder Willie sat down and sighed like Dolly Day-Dream. He let City have another chance, and they were wise to take it.'

But this was just one, albeit extremely important, problem Manchester City were facing. Awkward choices were soon to be forced upon them.

The club's ambitions to win a League title or the FA Cup clashed with a narrow parochial outlook held by certain members of the City directorate. The facilities at Hyde Road were still little more than primitive at a time when spectators endured more privations than would today's public. There was no protection against wind and rain anywhere on the ground, and few seats were to be had. To enter the ground, one had to scramble over a muddy bank behind the Hyde Road Hotel and trudge through more mud beneath a railway arch to reach the turnstiles. Changing facilities for the teams had for a long time been in a tent, and the opposition often had to push their way through a hostile crowd to get on and off the pitch.

With the advent of First Division football, strenuous efforts to improve matters had been made. The old box-stand, erected some ten years previously with funds donated by Chester Thompson, was demolished and a new covered stand – 210 feet long with room for two thousand people – had been erected. New entrances were created in Bennett Street and more turnstiles opened beneath the railway arches. Special entrances were built to allow season-ticket holders easier exclusive access and they also had their own private bar. Dressing rooms were built, complete with Russian and Turkish plunge baths, together with a covered running track. Sam Ormerod, the secretary, had his own office, and even a telephone.

On 29 September 1900, A.J. Balfour, the club's patron, shook hands

Billy Meredith shakes hands with A.J. Balfour at Hyde Road in September 1900.

A page from early club fanzine 'The Hornet'.

with Billy Meredith before kicking off the match against Liverpool, and the new Hyde Road was declared officially open. Unfortunately, the new fixtures and fittings were only part of the problem of adaptation with which the club was faced. The team itself needed extensive refurbishing too.

It had succeeded in the Second Division largely through Meredith's peerless skills and numerous goals, plus hard-working support from shrewd older men like Di Jones and Jimmy Ross. But the two veterans could not be expected to continue for much longer, while many of the players who had helped the club gain promotion could never hope to be more than journeymen in a First Division that demanded superior skills.

The directors announced at the commencement of the season that they were quite happy with the team as constituted and that they would rely on finding talented local youngsters in the club's Junior Colts competitions held during the summer, to replace or cover existing first-team players. They were attempting to make a virtue out of a necessity.

All went well at first with three wins and sixteen goals in their first four games. Sam Ormerod was dubbed by the *Athletic News* the 'Wizard of Longsight' and could afford the smile of satisfaction that 'Nondescript' of the same newspaper found on his face as he surveyed the crowds flocking into Hyde Road. 'I really wish they would stop coming,' Ormerod said, 'or else we shall have to make more extensive alterations to the ground. We have taken £350 in season-ticket money alone thus far. Our accountant is taxed to the limit and we are contemplating another huge stand to take up the space at the Hyde Road entrance from the railway arch.'

But the run of success ended and, though City finished a respectable seventh, it was clear that new, talented players had to be found to replace the likes of Ross and Jones.

During the following season much of the attention of Press and public turned upon Meredith. His form was beginning to suffer and the critics were as harsh as they had once been full of praise: 'Jimmy Ross has been telling an interviewer that Meredith is the finest right-winger he has ever played with, not excluding Jack Gordon of the Old Invincibles. Of course, it is a matter of opinion and Ross is entitled to his; but mine is different. On his day Meredith well-fed and nursed is the most dangerous and brilliant player, but he doesn't like donkey-work and if his partner is off, Meredith is off too. The worst of it is that, with Meredith off colour, there doesn't seem to be much stuffing left in the City attack – not even when Ross is playing.'

Meredith was the target for defences of a considerably higher standard than those of the Second Division, defenders who were not afraid to use rough tactics to hold him. He began to react to such treatment by lashing back, earning himself yet more criticism. Yet it was clear that once the threat Meredith posed had been nullified, Manchester City were helpless. In March 1901, a letter from Tom Watson, Liverpool's manager, was read out to an emergency meeting at City, denying that a Liverpool director had said, during a match between the two clubs, that 'all that the opposition had to do was watch Meredith – the rest are no good.'

When the announcement of his wedding had been made, journalists took the opportunity to poke a little more fun at City's perennial problem: 'William Meredith, City's crack outside-right and probably the cleverest man in his position throughout the United Kingdom, was married to a Miss Negus in the early part of last week. His masters

RUN DRY.

Meredith: It's very funny. I can't get anything at all now – look you!

have tried desperately to provide a suitable partner for the Chirk man throughout the season. Meredith, let us hope, has now solved this "knotty" problem.'

As Manchester City struggled into their third season in Division One, football disaster and even financial doom seemed inevitable. They lost thirteen of their first twenty games and won only three. During those twenty games Ormerod used twenty-nine different players, almost three full teams! What was most galling to Press and public was the fact that a lot of money was now being spent, but on poor players.

'Harricus', for *Athletic News*, sought Ormerod out at the end of September 1901: 'I had a chat with Sam Ormerod on Friday afternoon; the City secretary is one of the old originals of Lancashire football and a capital referee in his time. Manchester's lowly position formed, of course, the chosen topic for conversation. The genial Sam thinks his club is the victim of circumstance inasmuch as four of the five matches have been played away from home and, being thus handicapped as no other club is, he could hardly be sanguine of success at Nottingham but he thinks City's time will come. When I took him to task on the week-to-week chopping and changing of the team he said that personally he wasn't in favour of it, but what with letter writers and others, the lot of the directors wasn't a happy one, and no-one was more anxious than they were that City should rank with the best.'

A month later, nothing apparently having changed for the better, the same correspondent returned to the attack: 'A greater monument to folly and incapacity than the figure of Manchester City this season we have rarely seen. There was a time when we thought the shafts of satire and ridicule would rouse the club to action. But they have availed not. It is quite time the shareholders held a mass meeting and particularly invited the directors and officials. What is Mr. Ormerod doing? IS ANYBODY DOING ANYTHING?'

Another month, and the attack was taken even further: 'We neither see nor hear of displays of acumen, enterprise and business activity by the directorate and their servants. Two men are badly needed at Hyde Road – one shrewd and commanding personality with the ability to put the finances on the sound basis they ought to be, and to see that affairs are conducted in a business-like manner, and another is a shrewd and sound judge of a player and especially of a budding foot-baller.'

Behind the scenes, it was clear, a struggle was taking place between those who saw the need to reform the club's cumbersome financial structure so as to give more power to one or two men at the top who could rebuild the City club entirely; and those who were reluctant to face such a choice and who felt that the club could muddle through as it always had done.

The latter group, having been in control for the previous three seasons, were now held responsible for the chaos into which City had been plunged. The need for new blood was obvious, as was the need for a large injection of capital.

Prominent among the 'expansionists' was John Allison, a successful businessman who had left the City board some years earlier to concentrate on his hydropathic establishment. Manchester City's promotion to the First Division had provided Allison with some excellent commercial opportunities. The official club programme had carried advertisements for his baths together with gossip about the prominent sportsmen – footballers in particular – who had received treatment there. It had also advertised his *Football Results Telegraph* and in 1898 had even carried his election address when he had stood for the local council. Posters and handbills had clearly identified him with the club; he had been unsuccessful at first but now, in 1902, he was a councillor at last. He was a self-made man who had great ambitions for the City club, and he was instrumental at this crucial juncture in the club's history in persuading Edward Hulton, the wealthy newspaper proprietor, to stand for election for the City board. Hulton was happy to lend the club money, and was also prepared to pay for players personally – if Allison recommended them. Allison had many sporting contacts in Scotland, built up through his sporting clinic, and he set about using them to good effect. Hulton, meanwhile, began sorting out the club's financial affairs. And so began, in the midst of a catastrophic season on the pitch, a rapid rearrangement of the club's affairs off it.

In February, Sam Ormerod was all but removed from his position. Several directors resigned and Allison moved swiftly into the transfer market. It was at this point that Billy Meredith seemed to become a crucial factor in the wheeling and dealing in which Allison had become involved. The seeds of future discord were being sown. Meredith recalled some years later that with City headed back to the Second Division, he was even more determined to leave: 'Celtic made a big offer for my transfer from City and it was touch and go whether I left the Irwell for the Clyde. The late John Allison was connected with both clubs and it was through him that the negotiations took place.'

Allison was indeed in close contact with Celtic, but he appeared more interested in buying players than selling them, least of all in selling Billy Meredith. And to many observers it seemed odd how many young Celtic players were being made available: 'Surprise has been expressed at the Parkhead management releasing McOustra who has throughout the season given such rich promise in almost every position he has filled.'

There were others – Drummond, another young player at outside-left, and later Davidson, a full-back. There is more than a suspicion that Allison used Meredith as bait to tempt Willie Maley, Celtic's manager, to part with some promising players. Allison played a waiting game, settling with Meredith at the last possible minute: 'The Manchester club only agreed to my request just in time or I should have been over the border alright. . .'

Yet there is little evidence that Meredith received a great deal more than he was already being paid. His own account of his weekly pay suggests that, since entering the First Division, he had been receiving £6 a week, substantially more than the maximum of £4 then allowed, even taking into account possible bonuses. But it also became clear some years later that he was not the highest-paid player in the club – one of the new Scotsmen, Tom Hynds, received £6.10s a week. Perhaps Meredith had secured a date for a benefit. One was certainly planned for 1905. After eight seasons of remarkably consistent service, he had received just £40 by way of a benefit – half the receipts of a match played back in 1898. What is certain is that the vexed question of money would now become paramount in the affairs of the club and Billy Meredith in particular. Though Meredith appeared to respect Allison, he later came to suspect him of less than scrupulous motives in the handling of City's affairs. In fact Meredith came to feel that he had been duped: 'I have often thought that my career would have been more successful from a financial point of view had I joined the Scottish club.' Allison, Meredith noticed, never lost out financially. In fact, he often promised more than he delivered. He was able to get the best of all possible worlds in terms of business, politics and prestige – with little risk to himself if things went drastically wrong. However, a more immediate answer as to why the Celtic management were so amenable to Manchester City's requests for players (apart from the fact that Hulton was paying high prices for these men – £650 for Drummond and McOustra alone) was that Sam Ormerod's replacement as club secretary was to be Tom Maley, the Celtic manager's younger brother.

As Allison rushed to and fro, signing players during February and March 1902, Maley was seen at the City ground on more than one occasion. He was not unfamiliar with the older City hands – he had actually played a game for the club in 1897, and had received treatment at Matlock House, Allison's sporting clinic. With his arrival the famous Scottish connection that was to transform Manchester City within the space of a year was finally cemented.

Before anything else could happen, however, City had to descend once more into the Second Division. The new signings could not repair the damage done in the first half of the season.

At the club's general meeting in June, with relegation confirmed, it

Tom Maley

was revealed that Manchester City, although having taken almost £8,000 in gate receipts, were almost £1,000 in debt. The club chairman, John Chapman, a genial, gregarious man, took most of the blame. Hulton commented that Chapman was 'too kind-hearted to run a football club.' The club's officials had apparently spent money uncontrollably on travelling expenses, bonuses, wages. Sam Ormerod resigned and a new directorate was elected.

During the summer close season, a Manchester lad serving in the army in South Africa, where the Boer War had only just ended, sent Billy Meredith a gift: 'Opening it I found that my unknown friend had sent me a massive wooden spoon, evidently a good sample of the native art.'

Meredith decorated it with a blue and white ribbon and hung it on the wall of his bedroom.

4

Cup Triumph

'At last I saw the players run from the field and, at a word, our balloon rose and swung across the scattering throng, while a band played "Rule Britannia". I caught a glimpse of their glittering instruments and then, so rapidly did we soar, the grounds were spread out beneath us like a massive map. The stands were but half-peopled and thousands of tiny atoms were rushing across the ground and down the slopes to the grandstand where the coveted trophy was to be handed to the victors; it looked like flies swarming round a honey-pot, and other flies crawling up the broad path to the Palace. . . When we were three thousand feet and two miles away from the Palace, I could still see that mass of folk in front of the grandstand, but we were beyond the sphere of excitement, for below us was open country, and above the glorious sky, too beautiful for words. . . Gradually the haze and the clouds shut out the view, and the great glass house on Sydenham Hill became but a huge diamond sparkling in the sun.'
Athletic News, 24 April 1904.

Tom Maley, Manchester City's new manager, differed from Sam Ormerod in several vital respects, but chief among them was the fact that he was not overawed by Billy Meredith's formidable reputation, nor was he swayed by the latter's demands to have his own way on the field of play.

Until 1902-3, Meredith had been, for both club and country, a talented player among lesser men. Jimmy Ross and Di Jones had been veterans, great players from another era (and by the start of the new

The English Cup.

OXO is repeating the successes of last season, when no fewer than 215 walkers trained and won on OXO.

In addition to carrying the 1st, 2nd, and 3rd men home to victory at the 50 miles' Lancashire walk on Saturday, the 16th April, 1904, the very latest triumph for OXO is the winning of the English Association Football Cup. The following letter speaks for itself :—

Manchester, 7th April, 1904.

"I have much pleasure in testifying to the sustaining properties of OXO, the 'City' team having used it regularly during the Season."

(Signed) **THOS. E. MALEY,**

Secretary and Manager,

MANCHESTER CITY FOOTBALL CLUB.

" Got It."

season both had met sudden deaths). Finnerhan had promised, but had faded. Thus it is hardly surprising that Meredith's tendency to dominate proceedings on the field should have at times proved counter-productive. The City programme editor had commented in 1899: 'Then again I don't think any good can come of Meredith's "lightning" charges. If a man takes the field at outside-right, by all means let him stick to the position. I grant you that exceptional circumstances crop up when it is advisable to make an alteration, but I could see none for the home team captain's tactics ere the game was many minutes old. Then again, why will he persist in dribbling among the heels of his comrades and semi-bewildering them as often as not by passing at unexpected moments.'

Maley expressed a preference for 'style' in football – Scottish style in particular – and he was an enthusiast for the close-passing combination game as against the traditional 'kick and rush' methods then still very much in vogue. Maley possessed a tactical awareness that had been lacking in Sam Ormerod and he chose players for his side who would be able to put his ideas into operation.

He first experimented with various young players at inside-right – the elusive 'partner for Meredith'. Eventually, after spending money on talented Scotsmen who somehow never seemed to succeed with Meredith, he discovered Jimmy Bannister playing locally. Meredith approved: 'Bannister was one of the best partners I ever had; very little, if anything, below the best. No partner ever fed me better than Jimmy did and during the whole of my career at the Manchester clubs he was, in my opinion, equal to any inside-right playing in League football. I shall always think of him as one of the cleverest and most unselfish partners I have ever been blessed with.'

Two more young, relatively cheap players were also 'discovered' by Maley – Sandy Turnbull and Sammy Frost. Turnbull was to become an important man in Meredith's footballing career. The City directors had been ready to send him back to Hurlford in Scotland – as an inside-right for Meredith he had proved ill-equipped for the fetching and carrying job required. But Maley had sensed a goal-scoring potential and tried him at inside-left. Maley's instinct was proved correct as Turnbull immediately began scoring goals in profusion.

Frost, bought cheaply from Millwall a season before Maley's arrival, was a small, unlikely-looking inside-forward (yet another of

Jimmy Bannister (left) was 'one of the best part-ners I ever had', according to Meredith. A contemporary cartoonist (below) attempts to illustrate the 'Snowball' Frost tackling tech-nique.

FROST ROBS WOOD

those tried and found wanting at inside-right) and so Maley tried him at right-half and again success was immediate. He was, for his time, an unorthodox player. *The Newcastle Football Leader* said: 'Frost at half-back is unique. As a tackler he is a positive "original". Along comes the opponent with the ball. Does Frost put out a boot on either side? Not he. His *modus operandi* is far more certain and far-reaching. The ex-Millwallian simply throws himself across and in front of his opponent. "You can go along as far as you like" quoth Frost, "but you will have to take me with you". Small wonder that some people assert that Frost will get himself killed someday.'

Within the space of a few months, Maley had solved all the problems poor Sam Ormerod had struggled for years to resolve. Meredith now had a partner, plus a ball-winning half-back behind him to supply the ball, and a second lethal target to aim for in the penalty-area. But more than that, he had encouraged everyone else in the team to play a more sensible game – that is, not to simply funnel the ball out to Meredith and hope that he could continue to produce miracles. This more constructive approach was epitomised in Tom Hynds, another Celtic Scot who had also arrived at the club a season before Maley: 'Tom Hynds, the schemer, does not allow the captain to be fed too much. Rather it is Gillespie who receives the ball far forward and he either rushes or passes to Livingstone or some other player. I expect the idea is to draw attention from Meredith who seems to be a special mark for backs and half-backs.'

With a dashing young left winger, 'Tabby' Booth, to provide goals and ideas on the left, the Manchester City team proved too powerful for the Second Division in 1902-3 – in a twenty-match spell between 26 November and 14 April they lost only once and scored seventy goals.

As the 1903-4 season began, the changes in personnel continued as more of Hulton's money was spent on securing 'class' players. Herbert Burgess was signed and was destined to win an England cap within six months. S.B. Ashworth, a talented amateur half-back, was brought into the team to replace the injured McOustra. And Meredith was supplied with another partner, yet another Scot who had played for Celtic as well as Hearts, Liverpool and Sunderland – George Livingstone.

Commented the *Athletic News*: 'George Livingstone disdains style. He is all utility and a resolute thrusting forward who not only creates openings for Meredith but opens out the game by playing passes to the other wing in the style I used to admire when J. Devey was commander-in-chief of Aston Villa. He makes himself the hub of the game when he is on the ball.'

By December 1903, Manchester City were leading the First Division and playing with great verve and confidence: 'They move with a smartness and precision which could not fail to evoke admira-

Athletic News, January 1903.

tion, the forwards sweeping along like one man brooking no resistance. Small Heath's backs and half-backs never knew what was going to happen next; now a feint, now a pass, now a short dribble, maybe a shot or a wide pass to the wings, to be followed by a true, insidious centre – all these moves were executed with a perfect understanding and with clockwork precision.'

By now, 'special training' was a weekly occurrence; the players would spend two or three days cloistered away at various hydros, all paid for by the directors, and looked over by Maley and trainer, Jimmy Broad. Broad wrote: 'It was a real pleasure to train that team. They were all as keen as mustard and always to be found together. . . Tom Maley, who understands players perfectly, was always on the best of terms with his team and joined in any fun that was going on. At our sing-songs, Tom usually contributed a recitation and he did very well too. Turnbull, I think, was our best vocalist but McOustra and H. Burgess ran him pretty close for that honour. Jack Hillman was past master at making 'stump' speeches. When asked to do something serious he invariably settled back in his chair, lit his pipe and rolled out the tale of 'Young Lochinvar'. Billy Meredith spent most of his leisure-time enjoying the efforts of others. Bill was always very quiet when the others were giving an impromptu concert, but Bill relished it all the same.'

Whether the players enjoyed such monastic sojourns as much as Broad seemed to think they did was debateable. Meredith made it clear a couple of years later that he, for one, did not. The life of a professional footballer, he wrote, was not all pleasure: 'If he is married he has to say goodbye to many of the pleasures of home life and at the festive time of the year when everyone returns to meet round the family circle he is probably hundreds of miles away, perhaps shut up in some deserted seaside resort, undergoing special training for the purpose of providing entertainment for the more favoured members of society.'

With the possibility of real success being achieved by Manchester City, the restrictions the club felt it necessary to place upon its valuable charges intensified. For Meredith, a mature player in his late twenties, married with a young daughter, and quite capable of looking after himself and keeping to the strictest of routines, the constant shepherding about by club officials and 'trainers' was bound to irritate

Herbert Burgess (left) joined dashing left-winger 'Tabby' Booth (right) in the newly-promoted City team of 1903-4.

him. As for the special training itself, Meredith was never less than disdainful. In *Football Chat*, in December 1903, Jimmy Broad outlined the sort of activities the City team would engage in during a typical week away by the sea. The serious work would begin on the Tuesday after arrival. From seven o'clock until seven-thirty, the players would take a short stroll before breakfast, 'in order to fill their lungs with fresh air'. Fresh air equalled pure blood which increased their strength, according to Jimmy. Breakfast was a substantial meal – fish, chops, and other dishes. Then followed some relaxation, billiards usually, until ten o'clock. A six mile 'sharp' walk then ensued followed by hot sea-water baths, cold shower baths, brisk rubbing and massaging. Then dinner – soup, fish, meat, a great deal of fruit. An hour's 'siesta' preceded skipping exercises at three o'clock. These were followed by a substantial tea. After this it was 'early to bed'. On Wednesday some ball practice was inserted into the routine, shooting in at goal etc., and after the walk, punch bags, skipping ropes (Broad had originally been a boxing coach). On Thursday and Friday, they

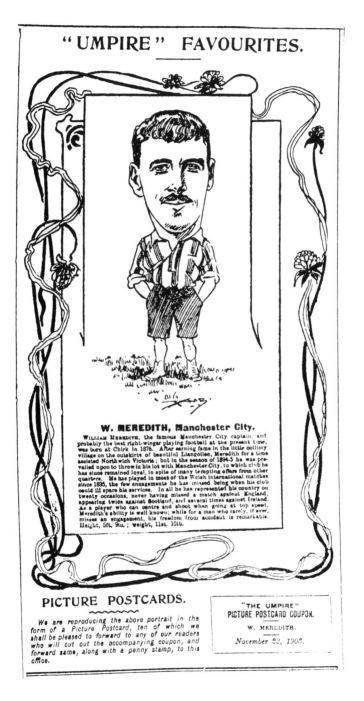

From the Umpire Sunday newspaper.

would take gentle exercise. But when asked by Frank Swift some fifty years later, whether they had done any special FA Cup training, Meredith replied: 'Yes, they took us to Norbreck and Buxton but I always thought it a waste of time. Still do. Had to go for long walks to stop stiffening up in armchairs.'

For the next few months, however, any disgruntlement he might have felt was to be stifled as both he and Manchester City careered towards those twin glittering prizes – the FA Cup and the First Division trophy.

In January 1904, Manchester City were drawn against Sunderland in the first round of the FA Cup. Until this season, City's record in the Cup had been negligible – they had never advanced beyond the second round. But this season their supporters were expecting something different. Sunderland were a powerful side. In the last four seasons they had finished third, second, first and third in the League. Thus, an excited and noisy 23,000 crowd greeted the teams as they stepped on to Hyde Road's greasy turf and, in a fast and furious match, City won 3-2. Surrounded by such an efficient, well-balanced side, Meredith produced one of his finest performances.

The *Athletic News* reported: 'The City captain was the raider-in-chief and undoubtedly the most dazzling forward on the field. Assiduously supplied, the famous Welshman hardly ever failed to respond to the calls made upon him. His command of the ball as he threaded his way through the maze of his adversaries commanded admiration. Against a team of such class Meredith has not often given a more dazzling display. R.J. Jackson, hard worker as he is, was quite unable to hold him in check and Rhodes, who has probably not seen Meredith before and knows not his wary antagonist, was altogether floundering about like an inexperienced schoolboy. I have no wish to be guilty of exaggeration, but Meredith was the King of the Realm.'

The *Newcastle Football Mail* reporter thought he knew the secret of the team: 'You'll ask the reason for Manchester's rise and I'll venture it in one word – grit. Class, as represented by the capture of well-known and expensive experts, is an almost unknown commodity in the team. Yet class, as represented by grafting, by zeal and strenuous endeavour and by the "git-tharism" which wins games when the footing of Euclid's problem fails, is literally bubbling all over the team from stem to stern.'

Athletic News, *8 February 1904*

HAS CITY DONE IT?

Manchester Evening News, 20 February 1904.

In the second round, Manchester City went to London to defeat Woolwich Arsenal 2-0 at Plumstead. George Robey, the famous comedian, took the team on a tour of London's music-halls before they were whisked back to the seclusion of Norbreck Hydro – quite suddenly, the season had picked up pace with vital League games following close on the heels of Cup games and, for some such as Meredith and Burgess, international matches.

In the Cup quarter finals, Middlesbrough were the opponents at Hyde Road and they surprised everyone by forcing a goalless draw. The replay on the following Monday almost closed Middlesbrough as factories shut down, schools had a half day and the majority of the Town Council had seats in the grandstand. But City won 2-1. Back in Manchester, crowds who had gathered outside the telegraph offices hurried off to spread the news: Manchester City were just one match away from Crystal Palace!

The meeting between Manchester City and Sheffield Wednesday in the semi-final at Goodison Park was a perfect clash of contrasting talents. Wednesday were the reigning Football League champions. Captained by England half-back Tom Crawshaw, they had built a successful side on solid defence. Though they had scored some sixteen fewer goals that season than City, they had also conceded seventeen fewer. Manchester City, Second Division champions, unbeaten in almost two months, were led by the country's most exciting winger. Thus, the question posed by the *Athletic News* was obvious: 'Would brilliant attack overcome solid defence or would the latter wear down the most persistent peppering?'

The day was overcast and wet; 50,000 people packed themselves into Goodison Park ('Need I say anything of pouring rain, packed cabs. sardined trains?' wrote Jimmy Catton) their cheers mingling with the strains of the St. Joseph's Industrial School Band, who now followed City everywhere on the big occasions.

And, from the very start, City's attack overwhelmed Wednesday. They were ahead after twenty-one minutes through Gillespie bundling in a goal after Meredith's shot had hit the crossbar; and two up at the interval, Turnbull having hooked in another Meredith cross.

In the second half, Wednesday attacked briefly but were broken by a third City goal twenty-three minutes from time. Turnbull again scored, inevitably from another Meredith cross. Meredith remembered it as quite the best goal he had ever seen: 'I never saw anything like it. I had centred square and "Sandy" took the ball first time when it was well off the ground and drove it into the net with marvellous force. The amazing thing was that the ball kept low all the way. You will understand the pace of the shot when I say the ball hit the net at Goodison Park and came out while the goalkeeper was still tumbling. . .'

Jimmy Catton praised the whole City team, Meredith in particular: 'Justice compels me to say that, in a fine and cunning line of forwards, Meredith stood out boldly against the skyline as the unapproachable artist. He was magnificently supplied by that thrusting, hard-working partner Livingstone, and by the indefatigable Frost, but he made the most of his opportunities by his dextrous dribbles, his teasing centres and his drives into goal. It cannot escape attention that all the three goals came from Meredith's play, although the finishing touches were left to others. No man has ever had a command of the "sliddery sphere" as Meredith, and it happens that no-one could hold him on

IS IT LANCASHIRE'S LUCK?

Never have two Lancashire clubs competed in the Association Cup final. Manchester City and
Bolton Wanderers are, however, determined to establish a record.
Manchester Evening News, 19 March 1904.

this, to him, memorable day. . .'

On the Monday following the semi-final, Jimmy Catton was in Wales for an international match. He entered Bangor Cathedral to pass a few moments: 'Lingering in front of a monument to a famous Welsh chieftain whose name, if memory serves me, was Owen Glendower, an aged verger walked up and desired to explain all there was to be seen. Gladly would I have availed myself of his services but I had to tell the old gentleman that this was a hasty visit as I must away to a football match. 'Oh,' said the verger, 'Yes – the game between Wales and Ireland. Ah, then you must have come from afar to see the great Me-re-dith,' with the central syllable stressed, accentuated long and the 'r' mellifluously rolled. Nearly did I lose my breath for never could anyone have imagined that the venerable appendage to the sacred building have ever heard of "Me-re-dith". One never knows what these quaint old personages, who seem so utterly other worldly, do understand. It is well to be careful.'

With the approach of the Cup Final, Billy Meredith's national fame

Athletic News, 21 March 1904.

was to be affirmed in a variety of ways. In March, the Manchester-based Sunday newspaper, the *Umpire*, announced the results of its poll to find the country's most popular player. Billy Meredith was the clear winner by over 2,000 votes. He received a £10 prize. Two weeks before the Final, the Grand Central Railway produced a prophetic poster-drawing to advertise its Cup Final excursions to London, showing Meredith scoring the winning goal. And an Oxo advertisement after the match showed Meredith holding up a cup of the steaming drink alongside a testimonial from Maley. How much Meredith and Maley were paid is not known, but Meredith's image was now as familiar as that of politicians and music-hall stars in an age when photographs had only just begun to transform the popular Press.

In the sporting Press, writing odes to Meredith (and other stars) had long been a popular pastime. For the Cup Final he was dubbed 'Will o' the Wisp' in a poem, the final verse of which ran:

> *He's a darling, he's a duck, is Meredith,*
> *And a mascot, too, for luck, is Meredith,*
> *Though ten casualties we own*
> *Still we don't break down and moan*
> *He can play teams quite alone, can Meredith.*

More poignant were the songs sung on the terraces by the young men of working-class Edwardian England – machine-minders, factory apprentices, clerks, the flotsam and jetsam of Manchester's industrial sprawl. . .

> *Oh I wish I was you Billy Meredith*
> *I wish I was you, I envy you, indeed I do!*
> *It ain't that you're tricky with your feet,*
> *But it's those centres that you send in*
> *Which Turnbull then heads in,*
> *Oh, I wish I was you,*
> *Indeed I do*
> *Indeed I do. . .*

But such adulation for mere sportsmen was too much for veteran players and journalists, even for such as J.J. Bentley of the *Umpire* who

FOOTBALL COMPETITION
RESULT.

MEREDITH, BLOOMER, AND CROMPTON CAPTURE THE PLAYERS' PRIZES.

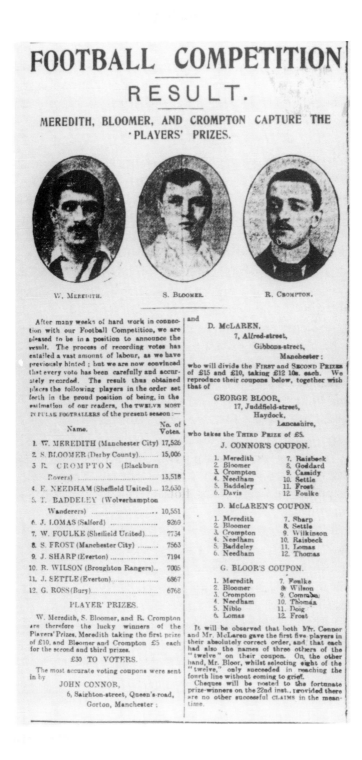

W. MEREDITH.   S. BLOOMER.   R. CROMPTON.

After many weeks of hard work in connection with our Football Competition, we are pleased to be in a position to announce the result. The process of recording votes has entailed a vast amount of labour, as we have previously hinted ; but we are now convinced that every vote has been carefully and accurately recorded. The result thus obtained places the following players in the order set forth in the proud position of being, in the estimation of our readers, the TWELVE MOST POPULAR FOOTBALLERS of the present season :—

Name.	No. of Votes.
1. W. MEREDITH (Manchester City)	17,526
2. S. BLOOMER (Derby County)	15,006
3. R. CROMPTON (Blackburn Rovers)	13,518
4. E. NEEDHAM (Sheffield United)	12,630
5. T. BADDELEY (Wolverhampton Wanderers)	10,551
6. J. LOMAS (Salford)	9269
7. W. FOULKE (Sheffield United)	7734
8. S. FROST (Manchester City)	7563
9. J. SHARP (Everton)	7194
10. R. WILSON (Broughton Rangers)	7005
11. J. SETTLE (Everton)	6967
12. G. ROSS (Bury)	6768

PLAYER' PRIZES.

W. Meredith, S. Bloomer, and R. Crompton are therefore the lucky winners of the Players' Prizes, Meredith taking the first prize of £10, and Bloomer and Crompton £5 each for the second and third prizes.

£30 TO VOTERS.

The most accurate voting coupons were sent in by

JOHN CONNOR,
6, Saighton-street, Queen's-road,
Gorton, Manchester ;

and

D. McLAREN,
7, Alfred-street,
Gibbons-street,
Manchester ;

who will divide the FIRST and SECOND PRIZES of £15 and £10, taking £12 10s. each. We reproduce their coupons below, together with that of

GEORGE BLOOR,
17, Juddfield-street,
Haydock,
Lancashire,

who takes the THIRD PRIZE of £5.

J. CONNOR'S COUPON.

1. Meredith	7. Raisbeck
2. Bloomer	8. Goddard
3. Crompton	9. Cassidy
4. Needham	10. Settle
5. Baddeley	11. Frost
6. Davis	12. Foulke

D. McLAREN'S COUPON.

1. Meredith	7. Sharp
2. Bloomer	8. Settle
3. Crompton	9. Wilkinson
4. Needham	10. Raisbeck
5. Baddeley	11. Lomas
6. Needham	12. Thomas

G. BLOOR'S COUPON.

1. Meredith	7. Foulke
2. Bloomer	8. Wilson
3. Crompton	9. Comrade
4. Needham	10. Thomas
5. Niblo	11. Doig
6. Lomas	12. Frost

It will be observed that both Mr. Connor and Mr. McLaren gave the first five players in their absolutely correct order, and that each had also the names of three others of the "twelve" on their coupon. On the other hand, Mr. Bloor, whilst selecting eight of the "twelve," only succeeded in reaching the fourth line without coming to grief.

Cheques will be posted to the fortunate prize-winners on the 22nd inst., provided there are no other successful CLAIMS in the meantime.

wrote on the eve of the Final: 'Since the City have become famous and especially as the Cup Finalists, it has been considered the proper thing to give every detail of their doings and I'm quite expecting to read that, while shaving, Meredith accidently came across a little wart and the great international actually lost ten drops of his precious blood. . .'

The city of Manchester, and Ardwick in particular, could not have been expected to share Bentley's scepticism. Manchester, for the first time in the game's history, was on the threshold of taking one of football's major prizes. In the week before the Final, preparations had been feverish. Public houses in the Ardwick area had closed down for the day and the patrons travelled down to London *en masse*, having clubbed together to organise 'picnics', the first arrivals sauntering uneasily from London's railway stations as early as Friday evening. But, wrote the *Manchester Evening Chronicle* reporter: 'The true character of the London invasion could not be gleaned until midnight and during the early hours of Saturday morning. At Euston, St Pancras, King's Cross and Marylebone, the trains, heavy laden, steamed in continuously. 'What a cheer!' I heard a jovial porter say, shortly after midnight. 'This is great, ain't it? Blimey! Did you ever see so many pubs in bottles? What, oh! Don't they grub?' And truly, the trippers upheld the tradition of the north. Each little party seemed to have brought their own stack of provisions for the weekend. Nine gallon barrels of beer, stone jars of whisky and big baskets filled with 'baggins' were almost as plentiful as blackberries in autumn, while there could never have been as many toastmasters on Euston station before. "Good Health!" rang perpetually in one's ears. "Hooray!" "Play up, City", "Here's to you, Bill!", "Good old Bolton!" '

By four o'clock in the morning the streets of London were ringing to the strains of 'Hiawatha' sung by the 'lusty-lunged boys of the Manchester Industrial School Choir'. Because of the early morning rain most of the supporters were content to remain inside the stations. All night trains continued to arrive, adding thousands to those already sleeping on benches, in waiting rooms, on platforms. Never before, so the railway companies claimed, had so many people been seen at one time on the platform at St Pancras. It was estimated that at least 16,000 arrived at Euston during the night on thirty special trains.

Eventually, at about ten o'clock, the clouds parted and the sun

shone, and the cooped-up thousands poured out into the city. Out at Crystal Palace people were already arriving: 'Some trippers, to be sure of accommodation, made their way to Sydenham as early as seven or eight o'clock. Those faded early-birds might have been seen sleeping peacefully in the Palace grounds. Later on, there were lively scenes at the railway termini of the companies serving Crystal Palace. The platforms at Ludgate Hill, London Bridge and St Paul's were packed. There was no place for regular travellers. "To the Palace to see the Cup", was the only cry.'

The teams had already been out on to the pitch late that morning and reporters had clustered round Meredith. The *Daily Dispatch* said: 'William Meredith, who like the rest of his colleagues, looks very bronzed, asked what his side's chances were, replied most emphatically, "Good. We ought to win". The Welshman is nothing if not cautious and takes nothing for granted. "You never know," he added, "but if we play anything like our normal game, the Cup is ours. All the boys are going for all they are worth. If today's game had been a

City directors and friends ready for the 1904 FA Cup Final. On top of the carriage (from left) are Lawrence Furniss, Josh Parlby, J.J. Bentley and Sam Ormerod. Director G. Madders is second from the left in front of the carriage.

League match, it would have been a pretty certain couple of points, but this is the Cup Final and, well, anything might happen".'

Bolton were a Second Division side with no prominent players. Indeed, Boyd, considered their best forward, had already been ruled out through injury. Though Bolton were a hard-working, strong side, City were their superiors in every department. The fact that it had rained the previous night and that the ball would move quickly over the wet turf was seen as an additional point in City's favour. 'Let's play our ordinary game,' said the serious Meredith, 'and nothing will stop us. And I don't see why it should, do you?' And the City captain, never remarkable for his loquacity, fell into silence and seemed to be wishing that the battle was over.

Outside and across the slopes of the Sydenham enclosure, the crowds were gathering. The *Bolton Football Field* correspondent painted the scene: 'A saunter round the vast arena, an hour before the match started, revealed other London products: tipsters haranguing the circles of waiting ones; dubious ones risking the policeman by tossing small coloured bricks on to a part-covered mat while knots of gamesters backed their favourites in colour; tired ones snoozing away the hour with their backs propped against trees, fences and railings, risking rheumatism; Cockney vocalists and musicians "busking in the old sweet way".'

By the Palace funfair, a large, gas-filled balloon swayed in the gusting breeze, the words '*Athletic News*' emblazoned across it. Inside was the paper's 'Balloonatic' preparing to ascend into the sky to cover the game from above.

As kick-off approached, crowds of spectators rapidly increased, spilling across the Crystal Palace slopes. Down on the pitch, the St Joseph's Industrial School Band marched and played and within the pavilion the celebrities were gathering. A.J. Balfour, now Prime Minister, and patron of the City club all those years before when they had still been Ardwick; the Colonial Secretary, Alfred Lyttelton; the Postmaster- General, Lord Stanley. Fresh back from their efforts to regain the Ashes were Wilfred Rhodes, C.B. Fry, George Jessop and W.G. Grace. The world of entertainment was well represented by George Robey and Harry Lauder. There were military men, Members of Parliament – such gatherings at Cup Finals were now the rule – and no one wanted to miss what was one of the year's great sporting spectacles.

Back out on the slopes, the tension was growing. The *Manchester Evening Chronicle* was equally lyrical about the occasion: 'It was an animated throng, one in which the spirit of partisanship was appreciably more lively than was the case among southern people. The rink was fringed with thousands of ardent Lancastrians, every man a connoisseur. Nearly everyone was willing to back his fancy, win or lose; the dark and the light-blue favours were strongly reminiscent of the University Boat Race. Manchester City seemed to be the favourites as was only to be expected, but the average Bolton supporters had almost an adoring faith in the potential of the "Trotters"...

'The feminine element was well represented, and it was evident that many of the ladies, the majority of whom supported light-blue colours, were prepared to shout quite as heartily as were their masculine escorts. There were many entertaining discussions at the

The Premier
greets W.G.

birds-eye view

entrance with reference to the vexed question of camp-stools. The
authorities were adamant, and all such conveniences were tabooed.

'The ground looked in beautiful condition after the rainfall of the
previous day and there was no great amount of wind to make its presence felt on the course of the flying ball.

'Of course, there was the usual crowd wandering on the fringes of
the field of play and the tedium of waiting was relieved by the Crystal
Palace band, but away on the far terraces, behind the southern goal,
the famous Boys Band of St Joseph's were cheering on their supporters by spirited strains. As the time approached, the policemen in their
usual persuasive manner, expeditiously cleared the precincts of the
pavilion so that the teams could make their way on to the ground.
Several enthusiastic Boltonians were to be noticed with bright para-
sols and white-sleeved hats ornamented with trotters.'

While all this was happening in the bright sunshine, down in the dressing room, a sad decision had been taken. The amateur S.B. Ashworth had been selected in place of 'Doc' Holmes, who had been with the club since 1896 and who had played in both the quarter- and semi-finals. The latter was so disappointed that he threw his boots through the dressing-room window.

Outside, by the funfair, the *Athletic News* 'Balloonatic' was about to take off: 'An army of willing helpers came forward to help drag the machine from the filling ground to the spot on the rise above the cycle track where was the arrangement by which the balloon was to be held captive. Over the green lawns we struggled and came to our anchorage. My hopes were higher still, and I patted my notebook to assure it that it would soon be at work among the clouds. A great roar from the football pitch told us that the teams had entered the arena, and I sprang into the car to the cheers of the small boys who had voted our balloon to be a greater curiosity than a football match.'

Calmly chewing on his toothpick, Meredith led the Manchester City team out on to the Crystal Palace turf, the first time a Manchester club had reached the FA Cup Final. The Bolton team, in white jerseys, followed, while high in the trees that overlooked the stadium figures could be seen clinging to the branches like colonies of rooks, tiny arms waving.

Meredith won the toss and chose to attack the southern goal where the City supporters were massed. The whistle blew and the 1904 FA

Meredith wins' the toss.

89

Cup Final was underway. Inside the ground Jimmy Catton described the opening moments: 'Bolton giving motion to the ball in that beautiful weather which always seems to be vouchsafed for the crucial contest. For some time there was little to choose between the rivals, although the game was loose. Manchester were the more systematic and scientific, with the result that Brown and Struthers had plenty to occupy their attention and their feet. The Wanderers seemed only to have one desire, to ply Stokes with the ball, but that policy did not pay, for Ashworth and Burgess were very vigilant and persuasive in keeping Stokes and Marsh in hand. When the left wing had a chance, White made a clever left-footed screw which caused Hillman trouble. On one side we had science and a desire to carry fascinating movements to a successful issue, and on the other dash and bustle and long passing, but the latter method did not pay.'

Outside, the balloon was having problems getting off the ground, as the 'Balloonatic' explained: ' "Just as I thought," shouted Mr Spencer after the car had come to a terrific bump on the earth, and while the silken gas-bag swung about overhead in a most drunken fashion. Men rushed forward to hold the lunatic basket down while we climbed out, and a sky-splitting roar told me that I had just missed seeing the winning goal.'

Jimmy Catton had not, however: 'At the end of twenty minutes Livingstone made a long, swinging pass out to the right for Meredith, who forged ahead and scored practically without opposition. Struthers was left, and with only Davies to beat, the deed was done quietly but effectively. Bolton seemed to lag behind as Manchester played even better still, and when the interval arrived they were certainly entitled to their lead of one goal – if not more on the play.'

Had the goal been offside, as some people claimed? J.J. Bentley, president of the League and one-time secretary-manager of Bolton, stated quite emphatically that it had been. Jimmy Catton felt it had been close. Whatever the truth, it had taken the Bolton defence completely by surprise – mercifully there was no television action-replay to decide the puzzle; for years afterwards Bolton supporters would claim they had been robbed.

The second half was similar to the first in that neither side seemed able to establish a coherence to their play. The ball scudded and bounced erratically and the players found it difficult to control.

Billy Meredith outstrips two Bolton defenders at the Crystal Palace.

Though Bolton pressed hard, City had the game well in hand, though a number of harsh fouls were necessary to prevent Bolton's hard-working forwards breaking through. Catton felt City were content to hold on to their lead and save themselves for a crucial League match the following Monday: 'At least, that was my view of the situation . . . but in doing so they nearly lost the lead they enjoyed . . . the City allowed the Boltonians to drop into their stride and hence a lot of trouble and anxiety.'

Meredith ran into offside positions on purpose so as to waste a little time, but when on the ball it was he who caused the most trouble to the opposition: 'Struthers was so unreliable and so feeble when he was not hampered in any way that I concluded that he had quite lost his nerve and his play. Struthers has had very little experience of Meredith and possibly is not desirous of more. Freebairn tried hard to keep Meredith, the Manchester captain, in hand, but the task was beyond him, for Freebairn has reached that time in his career when he likes to play a bit, and then rest awhile, whereas Meredith is like "the brook", he goes on for ever and ever.'

As the final whistle blew, Frost rushed across and seized the ball before Hillman could reach it and the players raced for the enclosure

THE FINAL STRUGGLE FOR THE ENGLISH ASSOCIATION FOOTBALL CUP: THE MATCH BETWEEN MANCHESTER CITY AND BOLTON WANDERERS AT THE CRYSTAL PALACE. (See page 8.)

Daily Graphic April 25th 1904

Meredith with the FA Cup at his feet and his victorious team-mates around him. Back row (l to r): Tom Maley (secretary and manager), S. Frost, W. Gillespie, J. McMahon, T. Hynds, J. Hillman, S.B. Ashworth, J. Broad (trainer). (Sitting): H. Burgess, G. Livingstone, Billy Meredith, A. Turnbull, F. Booth.

as the crowds swarmed across the pitch to where the Cup was to be presented. In Manchester, at the Hyde Road ground, 8,000 people attending a reserve match gave a roar of delight as the Palace result was chalked up on a special scoreboard in the stand.

As the City team made their way through the back-slapping, cheering crowds of supporters to mount the stairs, Lord Alfred Lyttelton held the Cup ready to place into Meredith's hands. Meredith took the Cup, shook hands with the Prime Minister and the Colonial Secretary and made a short speech.

Later he recalled: 'I'm hanged if I know what I said in reply, but I am reported to have said, "I'm sure it has given me great pleasure to win the Cup." That is not what I meant to say, if I did say it. But, anyway, it does not matter. I guess everyone knew what I meant, and probably if I did use those words, they amused my hearers as much as they amused me when I saw them in print.'

After the match, members of both teams were entertained at a complimentary banquet in the Garden Hall at Crystal Palace, attended by various MPs and dignitaries of the Football Association, and presided over by Mr Leigh Clare, MP, who said, '. . . there were a great many people who thought the time spent on football and cricket and other sports was wasted, but that was not his opinion and he was sure he could say it was not the opinion of those assembled there that evening. (*Hear, Hear, Applause*) All our English games were merely a continuation of that education they had had at school and what they had witnessed that day between two great Lancastrian teams had proved one thing, and that was that football in particular brought forth all the good qualities of courage, good temper, good feeling, pluck and fair play – (*Applause*) all of which were required in a foot-ball match and all of which they had seen displayed that day' (*Applause*). . .

The toast having been drunk with great enthusiasm, Billy Meredith, the City captain, thanked the chairman for his kind congratulations and the company for their generous encouragement. The City were very proud of their victory and had enjoyed themselves immensely, he said.

IN POSSESSION

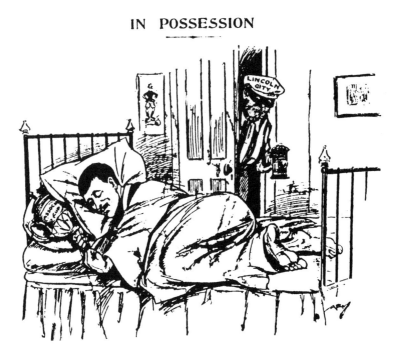

Has the burglar caught him napping?

5

'Football World Shocked'

'As soon as they caught sight of the trophy trimmed with blue and white ribbons which Meredith now and then raised above his head, they gave vent to prodigious cheering. Most of the windows of the upper stories were packed with people whose plaudits, added to by the blowing of a bugle here and there, and the music of the band, made a deafening sound. . . To the accompaniment of incessant cheering, the procession made its way at walking-pace down Dale Street where what might be called the welcome of the middle-classes was exchanged for that of the proletariat. It came from rough working men and larrikins and beshawled women and children in arms and hand, and was as hearty if not heartier than had gone before.'
Athletic News, 24 April 1904.

As the band struck up, 'See The Conquering Hero Come', Meredith must have thought he had reached the peak of his career. Never before had a Manchester club won that most coveted of trophies, the FA Cup. He had scored the winning goal, had been the club's inspiration for almost a decade. As Jimmy Catton had written a year earlier: 'Meredith is more a representative of his club than his confreres because he stands out almost as the player of the organisation, whereas others are, after all, sections of a complicated machine. Broadly speaking, but none the less freely, he brought the City within the pale of first-class football and he, with adequate support, would keep the club within the charmed circle.'

Directors John Chapman and John Allison used their City connections in their attempt to become Conservative councillors. Meredith, though his own politics were Liberal, later lent his image to the political cause of W. Millward, his business partner.

The events of the next two-and-a-half years would confirm that assessment, but not in the way the City club would have chosen. The turmoil into which Meredith was soon to plunge both the club and himself was not entirely of his own making, however. Though he was now a great man in his chosen sphere, he was not a free man, and his footballing life (and thus, almost his whole life) was controlled by others – men remote from the passion and elation of that triumphant homecoming.

The FA were finding the success of clubs like Manchester City hard to come to terms with. It was considered by many on the Council that the professional game had become so successful financially that there was a real danger of football's 'sporting' nature being lost irretrievably. Professionalism had long been anathema to the traditionalists who felt that only true amateurs could be said to be 'sportsmen'. But professionalism had been tolerated, particularly by those who recognised how much the game had improved from a technical point of view and, thus, aesthetically. And few could deny that the Football League gave much pleasure to vast numbers of working people. Thus, for two decades, despite the occasional celebrated 'poaching' case and much verbal snobbery, there had been little open conflict.

But the unresolved contradiction of professional football – that between a sport with its own ethos, being a mixture of class, educational and religious aspirations; and business with *its* own ethos consisting of profit, freedom of trade etc – was bound to surface sooner or later as the full potential of the game as a commercial entertainment was realised.

In 1900, the FA had accepted a resolution promoted by smaller League clubs and backed by certain County FAs, that professional players be paid no more than £4 a week, including bonuses. Only such a ceiling on wages could hope, it was claimed, to 'control' the professional game, could protect smaller clubs from losing their best players to rich clubs, could stem the destructive 'greed' of players who used the game simply as a means of enriching themselves.

That such a resolution flew in the face of 'natural' justice, indeed, of all the tenets of Victorian and Edwardian industrial Britain – freedom of contract, a workman selling his labour to the highest bidder, free market forces etc – seemed undeniable. But therein lay the inherent contradiction of professional football, which was to cause so much furious argument and produce so much bitterness over the next few years.

The ordinary conditions of the market-place could not apply to football, it was claimed, because football was a sport and its players were not workmen. Not so, the professionals argued. They trained and sweated and laboured and made sacrifices to produce entertainment for millions. Indeed, they argued, they were prevented by their clubs from doing anything less. They had families to support, a future to provide for. Thus, they were artisans, and ought to be treated as such, be granted rights as such. This, at its simplest, was the argument as it was to develop.

Inevitably, it would be overlaid by many other considerations – would become clouded and complicated by other factors: the undeniable greed for success and profits of certain League clubs, and the individuals who controlled them, combined with their duplicity in accepting the hold they had over players while still breaking the rules by paying them illegal bonuses; the distracting influence of class on many people's perspectives; the disproportionate influence of prominent personalities airing their personal grievances and pet theories.

Meredith's explanation for Manchester City's Cup success was typically blunt: 'What was the secret of success of the Manchester City team? In my opinion, the fact that the club put aside the rule that no player should receive more than £4 a week. From 1902 I had been paid £6 a week and Livingstone was paid ten shillings more than that in wages. I don't believe that any member of our team was paid less than I was, and the season we carried off the Cup, I also received £53 in bonuses for games won and drawn. Some players drew more. McMahon, for example, received £61 in bonuses that season. Altogether, the club paid in bonuses £654 12s 6d. The team delivered the goods and the club paid for the goods delivered and both sides were satisfied.'

There was a third party, however, who was not so satisfied. Within two weeks of City's triumphant return with the Cup, F.J. Wall, the FA secretary, and J. Lewis, a member of the FA General Council, came to Hyde Road and demanded to see the club's books. After a summer-long investigation, they could find no evidence of illegal wages and bonuses, but they did uncover discrepancies in the transfers of two men to the club – Frank Norgrove and Irvine Thornley. There were

Meredith's fame as a footballer allowed him to assume the role of businessman. His shop in St Peter's Square was destined to fail, like so many of his business ventures. Yet the shop sold many items that were bestsellers, including boots designed by Meredith, embrocations devised by him – even a revolutionary new rubber football. Later, his ventures into cinemas and pleasure boats were also to fail – only public houses were to bring him any sort of security.

cheques that could not account for the obviously forged receipts presented by the financial director; the FA committee therefore decided that the missing money had been used as illegal inducements, as signing-on fees far in excess of the £10 permitted.

In October 1904, Manchester City were fined £250 and the ground closed for a month. One of the players was suspended for a month, and three directors – Josh Parlby, John Chapman and Lawrence Furniss – were banned from football for three years. Mr Madders, director in charge of finance, was banned for life.

It was only the start of City's misfortunes. Meredith himself, at this point, was preoccupied with the sudden death of both his parents. He had missed a game (a rare event) in order to hurry to Chirk on the news of their illness, but he had been too late.

The 1904-5 season got underway. In January, the Cup-winning side were presented with gold-watches, the result of a public subscription to commemorate the historic win. Testimonials were promised to all the players – Meredith was to choose a match the following season. It was a prosperous time for him. The previous summer he had joined a sports- outfitting shop in St Peter's Square. Pilling and Briggs thus

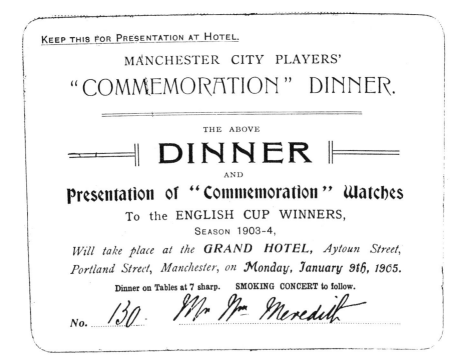

Athletic News Advertisement.

became Pilling, Briggs and Meredith. His name was used to promote footballs and football boots. In the shop window was a collection of his international caps and medals. His prosperity must have contrasted sharply with the thousands of Manchester poor and unemployed – 1905 was a terrible winter and many people were dying of malnutrition and cold. The Lord Mayor's Relief Fund was set up and blankets were carried round the Hyde Road ground for people to throw pennies into. Meredith helped organise a charity match with George Robey and his 'Team of Internationals' at Hyde Road. Robey presented the team with 'Robey medals'.

In February, Bolton Wanderers gained revenge for the Cup Final by knocking City out in the second round but, by then, City were engaged in a grim struggle for the First Division title.

By the beginning of April, City, Everton and Newcastle were separated at the top by just two points, with four matches left to play. City had a particularly tough programme. They had to meet Sheffield Wednesday, the reigning champions, then Everton at Goodison Park, followed by two Midlands fixtures, against Wolves and Aston Villa.

The match against Wednesday virtually ended their title hopes. Behind for most of the game, equalising through a Meredith goal in the last ten minutes, they seemed hesitant and unable to produce the dynamic flowing football of earlier months.

The following week they travelled to Everton, each side knowing that defeat would end their championship dreams. Newcastle had opened up a lead of two points and were looking far the strongest of the three. With so much at stake, the tension produced a scrappy, ill-tempered affair, culminating in an incident off the ball when Tom Booth, the Everton captain, flattened his City namesake quite brutally. Retaliation was inevitable, given the fiery temper of City's Celts, and when the teams left the field (Everton having been beaten 2-0) a police escort was needed to protect the Manchester players from the incensed crowd.

Undaunted, City went to Wolves and won 3-0. But Newcastle had dropped no points at all in their run-in, and they also had a far superior goal-average.

On the final Saturday of the season, City had to beat Aston Villa at Villa Park and hope that Newcastle would be defeated at Middlesbrough. If both sides won, Newcastle would take the title on goal average. Meredith recalled: 'Aston Villa had no chance of taking the honour. Our officials were very keen on us finishing with level points and we were offered a good bonus (£100) if we managed to do this. Our blood was up and the game wasn't the pleasantest.'

Villa were old rivals, of course, and City were never popular visitors to the Midlands. Their clashes with Small Heath over the years had never failed to end in some sort of trouble and, on principle, Birmingham crowds had a poor opinion of Manchester football.

As Meredith said, the Villa match was not the pleasantest. Villa, for their part, were in no mood simply to lie down and allow City to walk all over them. They had won the Cup the previous week and wanted to finish the season in style, an attitude the Manchester men seemed to find extremely irritating. By all reliable accounts City lost their heads in the second half. A weak referee, plus some over-zealous tackling, led to mud-slinging and eventually punches were thrown. The two players at the centre of the ugliest confrontation were Sandy Turnbull, never the most placid of men on the field, and the Villa captain and England international, Alec Leake, of whom it was said: 'With Alec Leake, football is a pleasure, a show, an unadulterated dish of delight. He will crack a joke with an opponent while he robs him of the ball.' Unfortunately, Sandy Turnbull was in no mood to swop pleasantries.

In the second half, with City trailing 3-1, the faint title hopes had gone. The match itself had already turned sour as the *Bolton Football Field* reported: 'Turnbull was in his dourest dribbling mood, dashing about with the ball with his whole heart set on victory. Leake found him a real hard opponent and, becoming annoyed at the rough impact, gathered up a handful of dirt and hurled it at the City man. Turnbull was not hurt and responded with an acknowledgement favoured by the bourgeoisie – thrusting two fingers in a figurative manner at the Villa man. He then says that Leake appeared to look towards the referee as though appealing, and not catching his eye, "gave Turnbull a backhander". The latter immediately responded with his fists and Leake was restrained by his fellow players from retaliating further.'

Predictably, the Birmingham-based *Sports Argus* saw the incident somewhat differently: 'To think that Leake, the mildest-mannered man and the most jovial who ever stepped on to a football field should be the victim of so unprovoked an assault as that committed by

Aston Villa player Alec Leake 'gave Turnbull a backhander', but no one could have dreamt the outcome of the subsequent enquiry which looked into the violence surrounding the vital end-of-season game between City and Villa.

Turnbull is entirely to make one's blood boil. It is a mistake to say Alec tried to retaliate after being struck once, as my correspondent seems to think. He had good-naturedly asked Turnbull, "what he was doing" on the first offence, thinking that it might have been one of the mishaps of the game, when the City sharpshooter struck him a second time. This was too much even for Leake's complacency and though George clung to his neck like the "Old Man of the Sea" and four to five other Villa players assisted the pacificatory efforts of the goalkeeper, Leake was with difficulty held in leash. This was not the last of the affair but I am not going to raise the veil that ought to enshroud the proceedings in the dressing room.'

'Last Saturday, Turnbull, after trying to fist the ball into the goal, banged the referee on the head.'
Sandy Turnbull was never the most placid of men and was regularly captured by cartoonists eager to illustrate his rough and tumble approach.

The match ended in a 3-2 win for Villa and as the players left the pitch, the police once again had to restrain the crowd from attacking some of the City men. On the way from the ground the City coach was stoned and reinforcements were called for to clear the mob.

It had been a depressing end to the season, and most of the players wanted to forget football and everything that went with it. Goalkeeper Jack Hillman left for America three days after the Villa match with a party of baseball and golfing friends while McOustra and Livingstone took themselves off to the Isle of Mull. Meredith, of course, headed for Chirk and the salmon fishing.

But the FA were unlikely to forget, let alone 'enshroud', what had happened. In the space of a week, three major clubs, challenging for the highest honours and prominent in the public eye, had produced exhibitions of foul play and violence that had provoked ugly crowd scenes and even uglier rumours. International players had been seen fighting and squabbling and disregarding appointed officials, none of which did the image of the game any good at all. What was possibly more significant, the clubs involved were to the forefront of the campaign to abolish the maximum wage. They were, even then, preparing their resolutions and circulars for the FA annual meeting, challenging, sometimes with embarrassing candour, the FA's right to impose financial ceilings on earnings. If the FA's authority was not to be undermined completely, it would have to take stern action: the professional game appeared to be descending into anarchy. Inevitably, a special committee was set up to look into both the Everton and Villa games.

What made the Villa case so much of an outrage was the allegation by Turnbull, prominently featured in all the newspapers, that he had been physically assaulted by the Villa players after having left the pitch. Once again, the *Bolton Football Field* was quick to produce inside information: 'Turnbull was coming off the ground (I think he was almost the first of the City players) and was going down the covered passage to the visitors' dressing room when someone, not a player, sprang out from the urinal and grabbed Turnbull, pulled him inside the Villa dressing room and the door was shut behind him. I thought the whole thing was in fun until, within a few seconds, the door was opened and Turnbull was pitched out heavily, by whom I could not see. He was yelling with pain and fright, and he had obviously been badly handled for his right cheek was grazed with a black mark or dirt (something like a cyclist describes as a cinder rash) and he had a mark on his ribs where he had been kicked (so he said).'

Though the Birmingham papers later conceded that Turnbull had, indeed, been attacked by the Villa players, they attempted to justify it. The acrimony increased. Accusations were hurled back and forth. But as summer arrived, the players dispersed. There were now only the rumours emanating from the investigating committee sitting at Derby. The *Bolton Football Field* again: 'A curiously significant remark was allowed to fall from Mr Clegg on the conduct of the enquiry of the committee at Derby. It was that, "the nature of the allegations could not be indicated at this stage". It was to ascertain what the allegations actually were and how far they were well-founded that the commission had been appointed.'

The mention of allegations came as a surprise to almost everyone. It had been assumed that the enquiry was concerning itself with the misconduct of players and inefficiency of officials on the field of play. 'Allegations' suggested something much more sinister, and the procession of players and officials from both City and Villa who filed before the committee merely added to the rumours. The *Bolton Football Field* was unhappy about the way the FA were going about matters:

' "Fishing enquiries" are not liked in legal life, but it is quite evident that the leaders of the FA recognise that there is a vast difference between the authority constituted by an Act of Parliament and that which depends on the suffrage of the associated clubs. Oaths would suffice in one, but to get to the bottom of things the FA must go about it differently.

'From what one can gather about the doings at Derby, the "fishing" was carried out with an amount of persistence and patience which would have put many an expert angler to shame. All sorts of bait – within the limits of the legitimate, of course – were brought into use, and some of those who were plied with questions as to the ultimate purpose, of which they were in the dark, have reason to fear that on more than one occasion they were caught.'

But no amount of criticism by the northern Press as to the FA's methods could deflect the commission from their course. If they were 'fishing' they were aiming to land an exceedingly big catch, while the waters in which they were casting were more than a little murky. And if anyone was going to succeed in such a situation, it would be J.C. Clegg, chairman of the FA Council since 1890, a tall, broad, grey-haired man who, according to a contemporary, 'as Official Receiver of Bankruptcy for Sheffield, has had a long and wide experience in the frailties of human nature. In matters affecting the honour of the game and the honesty of its control and management, his principles were said to be "nailed to the mast".

' "He turned me inside out, he did," it is said one misguided footballer, who left the committee room with the perspiration on his face, after a trying ordeal, remarked. "But he's as straight as they make 'em." '

J.C. Clegg, the FA chairman and 'as straight as they make 'em'.

On 5 August, after much feverish speculation, the committee announced its findings. By midday there could have been few newspapers to spare across the length and breadth of Manchester. Beneath banner headlines – 'Sensation in the Football World', 'Bombshell in the City Camp', 'The Football World Shocked', the news of Billy Meredith's suspension for attempted bribery of another player had been sprung upon an unsuspecting public. The relevant sentence in the report came at the very end: 'The Commissioners also reported on statements brought to their notice with regard to W. Meredith of Manchester having offered a sum of money to a player of Aston Villa to let Manchester City win the match. W. Meredith is suspended from football from 4 August until April 1906.'

It seemed to make no sense at all. What had the fracas at Villa to do with Meredith? How could an enquiry set up to deal with incidents of violence on and off the pitch, suddenly pass sentences relating to bribery? It seemed that all the midsummer Press criticisms of "fishing enquiries" and "secret courts" were justified, and the sporting

Press were to have a field day criticising the hapless FA officials on their mode of operation.

From his wife's home in Chirk, Meredith issued a vehement denial: 'I am entirely innocent and am suffering for others. Such an allegation as that of bribery is preposterous! I could never risk my reputation and future by such an action and I repeat that I never made such an offer. It is totally unjustified and grossly unfair. This sort of thing will demoralise Association Football. Manchester has not many friends among the Association officials and I doubt if the decision will be reversed or the suspension lessened if the whole case is reopened and enquired into. Had I been anyone but a Welshman I would have been better dealt with.'

Meredith's explanation was that he had merely congratulated Leake, the Villa captain, on his team winning the FA Cup. He would, he said, have been a fool to risk his whole career on a mere £10. 'The FA was too influenced by Aston Villa', he claimed. 'Manchester City,' he concluded, 'is becoming too popular to suit some other clubs.'

The immediate reaction on behalf of the public and Press was one of confusion. The FA had pronounced Meredith guilty, yet Meredith said he was innocent. Where was the evidence either way? How could justice be seen to be done behind closed doors? All was rumour and speculation.

The *Athletic News* printed a letter from an "Old International", summing up many people's scepticism, if not scorn: 'Why wasn't evidence allowed to be heard from Meredith? Why wasn't the public allowed to see the evidence? Why was Leake not suspended for the assault (with others) on Turnbull in the passage after the Aston Villa game? And why hadn't Leake brought his charges of bribery immediately, instead of waiting until a charge was hanging over himself?'

It certainly seemed inconsistent, to say the least, that while Sandy Turnbull had been punished with a month's suspension for his part in the incidents on and off the field, and referee R.T. Johns had been suspended for failing to control the match properly, Leake had not been mentioned at all. What added to Mancunian anger was that, in passing judgement on the events of the Everton v City match, when Tom Booth, Everton's captain, had clearly assaulted City's 'Tabby' Booth, the committee had seen fit to suspend the former's sentence, 'having regard for previous good conduct and the provocation received.' Turnbull had no such considerations taken into account. Perhaps, it was bitterly suggested, the fact that both Leake and Tom Booth were England internationals had something to do with their lenient treatment.

Meredith's rather bewildered response mirrored the confusion and anger felt in the football world at large at the handling of the enquiry. Given the terseness of the FA's announcement, and its determination not to discuss any aspect of its procedures, it was inevitable that speculation would run riot, for there was so much left unexplained.

The Birmingham *Sports Argus* did not help matters by revealing that the FA Commission had been 'impressed by what was told them by a disinterested witness who had overheard a most interesting conversation. The gentleman holds a responsible position in Birmingham municipal life and nobody would allege that he had concocted the story, so that all the hysterics from Manchester about being condemned merely on the evidence of a rival player may be treated with contempt.'

Not a mere player – but a gentleman! And Alec Leake confirmed that he had, at first, looked upon the 'bribery' offer as a 'joke' and had not mentioned it, but had been called back and 'forced to admit' to the allegation.

The FA's arbitrary power was now open to general question. It did not, it seemed, have to explain itself. It could just act and its victim possessed no right of appeal, no recourse to the established law of the land. On the evidence of mere hearsay, a 'gentleman's word', a player could have his livelihood taken away from him. It was 'the darkness of the secret tribunal, anonymous accusations and (as far as we know to the contrary) of accusations not put to the test of examination; in short, Russian darkness, the air whereof is alien to English lungs', according to the *Daily Dispatch*.

The truth was less sinister. The FA could not make its evidence public for fear of the laws of libel and slander. The FA's power rested on the acceptance of its judgements by all concerned; acceptance of its complete control over the game.

Attention turned to Meredith. Would he accept his punishment? Legal moves were confidently predicted; the Welsh FA was said to be ready to support him. There was even a suggestion that he would leave the established game altogether, join a National Football Agency run by a Mr Tagg, an entrepreneur who was trying to form an international eleven to play exhibition matches against foreign opposition – a clear challenge to the FA's authority. Meredith appeared, however, to be taking it all philosophically, as the Bolton reporter discovered: 'I strolled into Meredith's Athletic Emporium one day during the week and found the famous Welshman busily engaged in pumping and testing the leading "line" in footballs for immediate despatch. Business was indeed brisk and Peter Street will evidently fill in what might have been idle days for our "passive resister". Meredith confidently hopes that the Welsh FA and his club will be able to lift the cloud from around him, ere many weeks have passed, declaring his innocence earnestly and openly. As regards the "windy" canard Tagged on to a Birmingham report, his only connection with it is to express his readiness to go to Germany or elsewhere if the FA grant him permission. Which they will do unless the efforts on foot result in a reversal of his sentence. And then the club will claim him.'

At this stage, few people appeared ready to believe that Meredith had actually attempted to bribe the Villa captain. There was an air of mystery about the whole business, a sense that the truth had not yet been revealed. The FA's necessary secrecy played a part in that; Meredith's personality and reputation was also a strong factor and the *Athletic News* defended him: 'Anyone who has known the careful life and thrift which has characterised Meredith will feel confident that he never offered such a sum out of his own pocket. Where is the man who dare ask Meredith to try and purchase a victory and give him £10 for the nefarious bargain?'

But Meredith was not as calm as he appeared to be, nor as apparently idle. He was engaged in a bitter struggle with the officials of the City club, a struggle that was to burst into the open with catastrophic consequences: 'Though the FA suspended me, I felt strongly that my club would see that I was not the loser financially. At the beginning of the trouble it looked as if the club was going to recognise this, but later I found them shilly-shallying and putting me off until I got tired.'

Meredith was basing his confidence that the club would see that he was not going to lose out financially, on a letter he had received, sent by the club secretary, Tom Maley. Maley was later to disagree with Meredith's interpretation of that letter.

THE FOOTBALL ASSOCIATION, LIMITED.

Telegraphic Address:
" FOOTBALL ASSOCIATION, LONDON."

104, High Holborn,

London, 3rd April 1906.
W.C.

Mr W Meredith

Dear Sir,

Re Manchester City F C

The Commission will again sit at
the Grand Hotel, Manchester on Thursday
the 12th April at 3.15pm. Will you please
attend.

Yours truly,

[signature]

Tom Hindle, the FA auditor and 'the hammer of the professional footballer'.

Meanwhile, Manchester City had been forced to engage Tom Hindle, the FA's auditor, to keep an eye on the club's books for a season. Meredith's frequent appearances at the ground, his heated arguments with various directors and the secretary were impossible to miss. In February 1906, City were pressed by Hindle and Lewis to report the matter to the FA. The letter was written by Tom Maley and painted a sorry picture of behind-the-scenes events.

It read: 'I am instructed by my directors to bring to the notice of your Association the conduct of William Meredith, a player of this club at present under suspension. This player has been in attendance at almost all the principal matches at our ground and invariably frequented the dressing room and offices despite requests not to do so. . . . Periodically Meredith has approached the board for payment of wages. The refusal of the board to lend itself to any illicit or illegal practices led to many threats by the player . . . the rigid observation of the rules has ultimately silenced the player but nevertheless it has been for the board a very trying time. . .'

Another FA Commission was set up and by March, every City

MONDAY MAY 28. 1906.

COOKS IN CONFERENCE.

The CHIEF: "What shall the baking be?"

Athletic News.

player and official was involved. Meredith, it was said, was volunteering information that went well beyond the question of his present misdemeanours. He was claiming that he had been promised payments of specific sums if he held his tongue: 'The claims laid by Mr Meredith were stoutly denied and Manchester City promised to prove their good faith . . . in short, there is a nice kettle of fish.'

By April, the arguments had finished and the confessions had begun. The players as a body virtually cast themselves upon the mercy of the FA, as evidence of wholesale illegal payments – wages and bonuses in excess of those permitted – emerged.

On 4 June, the FA's report was published and Manchester City Football Club had all but been destroyed. Never had a club been so harshly treated. Several players were fined a total of £900 and all were suspended for a year. All the directors were suspended, Maley and chairman Forrest being banned for life. None of the players were to be allowed to play for City again and the club was fined £250.

Now began a bitter, acrimonious debate as to who was to blame. Meredith had been placed on the transfer list in May because, it was claimed, of his 'insulting attitude towards the board and because of his abusive language'. The breach was total and already Manchester United were said to have approached him.

Meredith was unrepentant. He remained fully convinced that he had been betrayed and that the directors had let him take all the blame and responsibility while themselves trying to hide behind the FA. The letter from the club was proof of their promise, he said.

But Maley had his own version of events. He was adamant that he had had nothing at all to do with the bribery attempt that had started it all, and he vehemently refuted Meredith's claims at the February hearing. The Welshman had then given up his earlier protestations of innocence, saying that he had, after all, offered Leake £10 to lose the match, but only at Maley's suggestion and with the full knowledge of all the City team.

Maley claimed the idea had been mooted among the City players, but that it had gone no further. Indeed, only three players had been involved and one of them had said that he would put his coat on before he would descend to such a thing. As for the illegal payments, Maley had found certain practices 'in vogue' when he had first arrived at the club and they were so business-like he assumed they were common practice. And the letter to Meredith? He had no ulterior motive in writing the letter – simply kindness and sincerity. When he told Meredith that he would not be the loser by his suspension he meant the public would remember him on the occasion of his benefit.

More hurtful to Meredith, however, were the comments made in the *Athletic News*: 'The famous footballer determined not only to admit that he had made an offer to Alec Leake – an offence which ought to have ended his football career – not only that he had been most lavishly and generously paid by the club which ran dreadful risks to give him all they had except the goalposts, but dragged everyone else he could into the same mess. No sense of gratitude for all the managers who, over the years, remunerated him so that he became comparatively rich, no ideals of friendship for the men who, admitting his enviable playing skills, had done everything they could for him, and no feeling of loyalty for the comrades who had fought side

City 1905, the team that might have ultimately brought the League title to Hyde Road. Back row (l to r): Broad (trainer), McMahon, Moffat, Mr Forrest, Hillman, Mr Davies, Pearson, Booth, Mr Maley (secretary). Front: Turnbull, Burgess, Jones, Meredith, Frost, Hynds.

by side with him in many a scrap of hard games restrained this man from divulging the secrets of his masters and colleagues. It would have been honourable to confess his own deeds, to express his sorrow and promise an amendment that he promised to fulfil but he took a course that amounted to revenge after he had been simply killed by kindness by the club whose colours he wore.'

This was too much for Meredith and, in a long letter to the *Athletic News*, he attempted to justify his actions. He calculated how much money he had lost.

Sir,

In your last issue there are a number of paragraphs in which you have labelled me disloyal and treacherous and have sought to stigmatise me in the eyes of the public.

You approve of the severe punishment administered by the Commission AGAINST ME and state that the offence I committed at Aston Villa should have wiped me out of football forever. Why ME ALONE? when I was only the spokesman of others equally guilty?

You state that in January, Mr Clegg asked Manchester City to report me. Since I was not reported officially until 14 February where and from whom did Mr Clegg get his information? Only Mr Clegg can answer this question truthfully. I suggest that Mr Allison had made a private statement to Mr Clegg compromising myself and this resulted in Mr Clegg's 'threat' and my being officially reported, and finally in the appointment of the commission.

In discussing my conduct you state that I was 'most lavishly paid'. I contend that I have earned every half-penny that I have received and I wish to inform you that my wages during the first five years of my connection with the club averaged under £4 a week all year round. For the last three years I have not been the highest-paid player in the club and to the best of my knowledge and belief I have never received any more for bonuses than any other player in the team.

You state that Mr Allison was not a director when Manchester City won the Cup. This is perfectly correct, but he was a director when, at the opening match of the season at Stoke, the team was promised a large bonus if they finished in the first six in the League. But he was not a director when the money had to be found, having conveniently resigned in the meantime.

I consider your criticisms neither manly nor fair. Have I not suffered for my misdeeds? I have lost:

10 months' wages (1905-6 at £6 a week) £258
7 months' wages (1906-7 at £4 a week) £116
FA fine £100
Loss of benefit match (City v Newcastle) £1,200

£1,674

Surely no one will believe that I ran the risk of incurring this enormous loss unless, as the official report stated: "The commission has come to the conclusion that statements were made to Meredith which led him to believe that he would receive his moneys after Mr Hindle had ceased to act. Further the commission reported that the chairman, secretary and the present directors made themselves party to irregularities etc.'

119

I deny that it was I who brought this trouble to the club and suggest that it was the chairman Mr Allison who was the primary cause of the latest enquiry.

Billy Meredith

But there seemed little regret concerning the bribery attempt. In fact he was never subsequently to offer a convincing explanation for it, nor was he ever to express any contrition. In 1919, for instance, this is what he wrote about the Manchester City 'sensations': 'One of the followers of the Villa club gave evidence that he had overheard a conversation I had with Leake regarding the result of the game. Leake was brought back and questioned on the matter. He admitted that I had spoken to him, but that in his opinion it had only been a joke.' Nothing more was added.

The *Bolton Football Field* was less harsh on Meredith, sensing that he was to be pitied rather than condemned: 'It has been suggested that some of the other players might not be so friendly towards him after the recent revelations. But it is hardly likely that he would refuse to answer direct questions put to him and scorn all consequences when he had been forced before the last commission by a report from his old employer. The players themselves realise he was obliged to be outspoken and the argument concerning them and Meredith won't hold water. . .

'Let me remind you that Meredith is no cunning astute financier or a sleek diplomat. A village youth, an artist at football and delight to hundreds and thousands of football enthusiasts, a maker of thousands of pounds for League and other clubs and Associations, a sober and consistent performer. . . Is it right that the club which he has made famous should at this juncture at any rate seem to be want rid of the trouble of him?'

Underlying all the arguments and accusations was the cynicism and hypocrisy of the professional game. It was common knowledge that wages of £6 and £7 a week plus bonuses were being paid to most top players and that they would continue to be paid. Meredith and City had simply been unlucky. As Meredith put it 'Clubs are not punished for breaking the law. They are punished for being found out.'

The bribery attempt was clearly a foolish, almost farcical episode, something someone with more judgement might have laughed away. Meredith, who appeared to have been influenced by some of his colleagues rather more than was good for him, increasingly appeared to be not quite the dominant, decisive man his playing image suggested. The very fact that he had been receiving less money than men who had been at the club for half the time he had (leaving aside his status in the game and his enormous value to City) speaks volumes for his relative innocence. It might also explain the anger and bitterness he felt – even bewilderment – and with which he expressed himself once the scandal had broken.

Even so, it is hard to view Meredith in quite the same brilliant light as that in which he had bathed up until the fateful April afternoon in 1905. All his virtues – his dedication, his abstemiousness, his abhorrence of the 'inhuman' transfer system, his sportsmanship on the field of play – were cast into shadow. Perhaps he realised that fact. His subsequent efforts to reform the professional game suggest a desire to create a more healthy environment – that is, a more honest environment – for professional football.

He must certainly have appreciated his luck in not having been banned from the game for life. Instead, the relentless football calendar turned again, the slate was wiped clean, and a new season beckoned. As 1906-7 approached, it was rumoured that Manchester United had signed him and that he was ready to take up their cause as soon as his suspension was lifted in the New Year.

City's shareholders were dismayed and angered to learn that City would receive nothing for his transfer. For once the tangle of documents, promises and secret negotiations had turned out to favour Meredith. City had signed an undertaking a year earlier promising Meredith a benefit match and a minimum sum of £600 (one of the main reasons why Meredith had pursued the club's directors so doggedly). The document placed a legal liability on the club and the FA declared it could force them to pay. Instead, Meredith said he would be happy with a free transfer. Manchester United, his new club, would then be more amenable to offering him a benefit match in a year or two. His career, he thought, was not likely to be a long one.

The truth, however, as revealed in his memoirs, was somewhat different: 'The City club put a transfer of £600 on my head. And United were prepared to pay it. But I refused to let them pay a half-penny. I had cost no fee and I was determined that I would have no fee placed on my head. The City club began to talk big and it seemed that I was going to be strung up again.' Then the benefit agreement came to light. 'I was prepared to fight the matter. The City club were not. I was given a free transfer and, as a result, I got £500 from a gentleman to sign for Manchester United and he also paid the £100 fine to the FA.'

In effect, Meredith had pocketed his own transfer fee, and some more besides. His lifelong aversion to transfer fees had paid off in a remarkable way. And his later demand that a player should have a share in any transfer fee paid for him was here realised beyond his wildest dreams.

The City club could have been forgiven for feeling they had come out of the affair the real losers. After taking close on £50,000 in five years, the club had now no real assets at all – no property, no freehold – just a few stands, some kit, and cash in hand of £15. 'Few football organisations have had such support and not one has earned such notoriety for football illegality and such shoddy finance,' wrote Jimmy Catton.

It was by no means the end of Billy Meredith's Manchester City days, but it was the end of Manchester City's first great era.

THE RESURRECTION.

Willie Meredith is endeavouring to revive
the Players' Union.

6

Meredith's Union

'As I say, it is a glorious opportunity, we must not miss it, or professionals are forever doomed. The FA think the players will weakly submit. I don't. We have waited our chance. It has arrived and we must decide once and forever whether the professional player is to be a man or a puppet in the hands of the FA. Do all you can for us by speaking or writing to others. . .'
Herbert Broomfield, Players' Union secretary, in a letter to all members of the union, June 1909.

One of the most unpleasant features of the Meredith-Manchester City scandal was the way in which professional footballers had been portrayed in the Press. Individual FA and League committee members had used their regular newspaper columns to call them greedy and had criticised the management of the City club for being weak, for allowing the players to gain the upper hand. One wrote: 'We cannot help feeling sorry that men of intelligence and of good reputation in their several walks of life should have driven a coach and four through the rules of the Association and been so generous to the players. The professionals have not been able to resist the impulse, the desire to obtain all they could from the club coffers.'

This condescending attitude towards the players was more than matched by the FA Council during the enquiry. A few years later, at the height of the Players' Union controversy, Billy Meredith wrote: 'Personally I really don't think that the gentlemen who sit on the FA Council have ever at all realised how absurdly autocratic, unfair and unjust has been their attitude towards the players. Ask any man who

NEW WELSH REVIVAL *Meredith: Friends, countrymen, players, lend me your ears!*
(Meredith has issued a circular advocating a Players' Union – an old scheme revived.)

has had to attend an FA Commission to tell you what he thinks about
it. They have always treated the player as though he were a mere boy,
or a sensible machine or a trained animal. When they were displeased
they just cracked the whip or gave him a slap. They had never
dreamed that the man might be able to explain things if he were given
a fair chance and that if he did give a good explanation he might be
man enough to resent his treatment if that explanation were merely
pushed aside with a contemptuous laugh.'

The Manchester City affair also confirmed for Meredith a number
of his own convictions and prejudices. First, that northern clubs and
Manchester's in particular, were resented by the Football Association
– 'Manchester has few friends in the FA,' he had said. Second, that as
a Welshman he had been victimised by the English because Alec
Leake, an England international, had escaped virtually unscathed
without so much as a fine to pay for his misdemeanours that day at
Aston Villa. Third, that as a simple player he had suffered dispropor-
tionately when compared with the various directors involved who
remained free to continue earning their livings, running their businesses etc while he was virtually unemployed. And last, that the

restraint placed upon his right to sell his labour in the free market as and when he chose was unjust.

It is surprising, given his 'radical' stance on so many issues, that he had played no part as a young man in the original Players' Union established in 1897, even though some Manchester City colleagues such as Jimmy Ross had been extremely active. That short-lived experiment had been scuppered in 1900 by the unilateral decision of the FA to institute a maximum wage of £4 a week – a decision that had been at the root of much subsequent trouble and scandal.

Meredith's politics were never extreme although he was an admirer of Lloyd George and always voted Liberal, or said he did. Having been brought up in a Welsh mining village, he certainly appreciated the value of collective action in order to secure what he understood to be a man's basic rights – in particular, the freedom to do as one pleased, to determine one's own course in life. But he was not a socialist as he has sometimes been depicted. Indeed, his views could almost have been said to have been elitist.

This was what he wrote in the *Bradford Argus* in 1908, commenting on the suggestion put forward by the bigger League clubs that all financial restrictions be removed: 'At last! At last the large cities and the biggest crowds are to have football of the best, and at last the players are to have a genuine inducement to show for the benefit of the public all the skill that is in them. The day of the man who is content to exert himself one week in four is over. Men will now be paid according to their ability and conduct. The best man will have the best salary, and as well will always have an incentive to try for more. The player who is not worth £4 a week will no longer receive it.'

The inherent contradiction of professional football – men being paid to play a game – no longer concerned him. He loved the game and it was his life. But as a professional he was forced to look upon it as work and himself as a workman. In an article entitled The Art of Wingplay, which he wrote for the four-volume *Association Football and the Men Who Made It*, published by Caxton in 1906, Meredith talked briefly about how to become a good winger or, more accurately, a good footballer, but the major part of the article is concerned with the social and professional status of players. When Jimmy Catton reviewed the book in February 1906, he noted that Meredith's contribution was not as 'practical' as those of other famous players writing on their various positions, which was a polite way of saying that Meredith had used the platform given to him to speak out about a professional footballer's life, his sacrifices and injuries, his worthiness to be taken seriously.

And it was this theme – the professionalism of the paid player – that he would return to over and over again. He wrote 'What is more reasonable than that our plea that the footballer, with his uncertain career, should have the best money he can earn? If I can earn £7 a week, should I be debarred from receiving it?

'I have devoted my life to football and I have become a better player than most men because I have denied myself much that men prize. A man who has taken the care of himself that I have ever done, and who fights the temptation of all that injures the system, surely deserves some recognition and reward? They congratulate me and give me caps but they will not give me a penny more than men are earning in the reserve team, some of whom perhaps do not trouble themselves to improve themselves and don't worry about taking care of condition. If football is a man's livelihood and he does more than others for his employer, why is he not entitled to better pay than others? So far as I can make out, the sole reason why the best footballers in England are prevented from earning better pay than men of lesser ability and experience is purely sentimental.'

Unfortunately, those 'sentimental' reasons were to prove considerable stumbling blocks. The sentiments of the times were tinged with fear and uncertainty on behalf of those who 'ruled' those below them in the social scale. This was the period of the birth of the Labour Party; no more than two years earlier there had been a revolution in Russia. It had affected men's thinking. At home, a reforming Liberal Government had passed legislation ensuring millions of working people damages in case of injury and misfortune suffered at work. It had also produced the Trades Dispute Act which encouraged and protected Trades Unions. In 1909, the year of the Players' Union's struggle to exist, strikes were causing disruption in industrial Britain. Miners rioted in Staffordshire, and Manchester itself was brought to a standstill by demonstrations of the unemployed, and striking transport and municipal workers. It was a highly-charged period in British history – emotions rather than cold reason were bound to predominate, and the Players' Union's demands. A number of professional

The League having forbidden the wearing of badges, the players may consider the above suggestion for signalling their membership of the Union.

footballers, for instance, were embarrassed by the sorts of demands Meredith was making on behalf of his fellow professionals. Many players saw themselves as a privileged caste who should not complain – particularly when looking out upon a world where, for the bulk of the working population, life was extremely hard. And there were players who continued to feel that the FA Councillors were their 'superiors', or who continued to exhibit a deference based on the disparity of class.

But Meredith was contemptuous of such views. Whether true or not, he was convinced that club directors and shareholders ('Those little shopkeepers who govern our destinies') were making large profits from football while hypocritically invoking the largely amateur 'principles of the game' whenever it suited them. As he pointed out after the scramble to secure his signature after the Manchester City scandal: 'The League met and the representatives of each club voted in favour of the punishment meted out to us being enforced. And while their representatives were passing this pious resolution most of them had other representatives busy trying to persuade the "villains whose punishment had been so well deserved" to sign for them under conditions very much better in most cases than the ones we had been ruled by at Hyde Road.'

As for the FA, his comment in September 1911, some years after the first great confrontation, summed up his attitude: 'The FA is an obsolete battleship and the League is an up-to-date Dreadnought. The haughty, snobbish idea will not now go down, because many of the present-day players are better educated men than some of the people who rule the game.'

Thus when he set out to re-establish the Players' Union in 1907, there was no attempt on his part to curry favour with his 'masters'. The Players' Union stated its aims – freedom of contract, access to the laws of the land, an end to wage restraint etc – and was not interested in persuading the Football Association (or the Football League for that matter) that their demands were right or justified. To Meredith and the union, the demands were common-sense, self-evident.

And at first, his proposals – contained in a circular sent to all professional players – were discussed amiably, if a little warily. The *Athletic News* – mouthpiece of the League – commented, 'William Meredith has received much advice – free, gratis, as if he were Simple Simon – and several answers to his circular asking his brother professionals their opinion as to the formation of a PU and most of them are in favour of the project. The majority of the men have not, however, replied. We cannot conceive of any player with a grain of sense refusing to support the establishment of a body for the protection of his own interests. Meredith's proposals seem perfectly proper and reasonable providing, as we understand to be the case, the Union were used as an instrument of defence and not without due provocation as an instrument of defiance.'

The paper was uncertain as to how many players would actually join, but said: 'Meredith, however, is distinctly hopeful. He argues that the player of the present day realises the serious side of football more than the player of five or six years ago. He hopes shortly to call a meeting of prominent players who are in favour of a union and to discuss the matter and decide a course of action.

'His idea is that the union, to be successful, would have to receive the support of the great majority of the professionals and would have to possess sufficient funds to establish an office and remunerate a secretary who, in Meredith's opinion, ought not to be a player. Meredith hopes to see the day when the players have direct representation on the ruling body. He says there are many matters that ought to be brought to the attention of the FA and he is convinced the members of the body do not realise the conditions under which players labour.'

Despite general scepticism, the Players' Union was swiftly established. On 2 December 1907, at the Imperial Hotel, Manchester, with Meredith in the chair, a meeting of representatives from over a dozen clubs established the basic machinery and in January 1908, at the King's Arms, Sheffield, the name was ratified: The Association of Football Players Union. J.H. Davies, Manchester United's chairman was elected President, and vice chairmen included John Cameron of Spurs, John McKenna of Liverpool, Jimmy Catton of the *Athletic News* and F.W. Rinder of Aston Villa. Moves were made to establish their position with regard to the new Workmen's Compensation Act. An office was opened in Manchester's St Peter's Square, close by Meredith's shop, and Herbert Broomfield, Manchester United's reserve goalkeeper (and a future business associate of Meredith's) was erected secretary. He immediately requested a benefit match in aid of the family of a player who had recently died and whose club was paying no compensation whatever.

In March, the rules were published and were seen by the *Athletic News* as being basically 'defensive' with much emphasis placed on the apparently uncontroversial idea that a player in need should be provided with financial assistance. But the main controversy continued to surround the discussion going on between the clubs and the FA concerning the payment of players – how much and in what form. All kinds of systems were being suggested: talent money, super-player clauses, complicated benefit schemes. In 1908 twenty top League clubs even threatened to form their own 'super league' if some flexibility was not conceded by the FA but, though the governing body was broadly in agreement with the idea of liberalising the existing £4 a week maximum, nothing could be agreed upon and stalemate ensued.

The Players' Union response (they were not represented on the governing body and were never consulted) was to stand aloof from the discussions and assert that no 'system' would work, that complete freedom from all restraints was the only solution.

The *Athletic News* thought this was a little too strong: 'We have no hesitation in saying that the sweeping aside of all restrictions in reference to money is solely the idea of a few rich clubs, of a few players, who are in a class by themselves. . .'

The words, 'a few rich clubs, a few rich players who are in a class

THE STEPPING STONE.

International Association Player: Come along, boys; it's an easy jump from here.

by themselves' was an indirect reference to Manchester United. Apart from Meredith, the United club provided the union with its chairman, its secretary, and the intelligent, articulate club captain Charlie Roberts, who would play an important part in union affairs in the years to come. League champions in 1908, Cup winners in 1909, they were one of the glamour clubs of the day and their general prominence and popularity were important factors in keeping the Players' Union in the news.

In December 1908, at its first annual general meeting, the PU declared that they wanted no restrictions at all on earnings they wanted clubs to be deprived of the power of retention after having offered the maximum wage; they wanted players to be accorded the right to negotiate their own agreements and to be awarded a percentage of any transfer fee. The *Athletic News* commented: 'We now know the ultimate demands of the players. They may be crystallized into one sentence: unlimited wages, with the right to move from clubs and share in transfer fees. These are the dreams of visionaries. . .'

For one particular man – C.E. Sutcliffe, FA Council member, League committee member – the demands of the players could be summed up thus: 'The strong feature of the whole resolution is self-interest.' There was, he was outraged to notice, 'not one word of loyalty to the FA.' It was the spirit of selfishness that was ruining the game and clubs before the maximum wage was introduced. He had, he said, wanted to help the players, 'but I can play no part in helping the players in immoderate and unreasonable demands.' He claimed that they were committing suicide, their resolutions were contemptible claptrap and, what was more, they were ignoring his and his League committee's wise council: 'We were running football years before some prominent players knew anything about it!' He concluded: 'The latest pronouncement of the PU is but the outward and visible sign of their inward greed.'

Until now, the argument had been an academic one. The union had no power to enforce its proposals. Many of the leading clubs were sympathetic with their ideas regarding wages and Sutcliffe's remarks were by no means representative of official opinion. But the climate was to change quite rapidly.

In February 1909, Meredith was sent off for the first time in his life, during an FA Cup match. He was banned for one month, a harsh judgement considering that he had never transgressed on the field during his many playing years. When, almost as a response to this, he wrote an article that appeared a week or so later, purporting to be an account of a dream he had had of the players going on strike, C.E. Sutcliffe could hardly contain himself. He wrote: 'What an optimist he is! He is only looking forward three or four seasons so he tells us. When I read the wonderful dream I thought it was a rich joke, but I was solemnly and publicly assured on Wednesday last by a member of the PU that they are all laying their plans for a strike three years hence. Meredith's picture of inadequate payments and scurrilous treatment, of empty trains and deserted trams, of public resentment and withdrawal of football editors is a cheery fantasy from a pro's point of view. I really grew alarmed until I got near the end when I found that the strike that had commenced on Saturday had ended in complete victory by Monday for the players.'

But suggestions of strike action, even in jest, disturbed the League clubs. They were already worried by the Players' Union's demands that when a player was in dispute with his club over wage arrears he should be properly represented by a lawyer and should be allowed to go to court under the new Workmen's Compensation Act. This, the clubs insisted, was for the FA alone to decide. In effect, they were saying that a professional footballer had no right to go to law. The union's response was emphatic: 'The Players' Union management committee are not convinced that they are expected to regard seriously the opinion that a footballer forfeits a common legal right on entering a professional agreement with a football club.'

It was becoming clear that a fully-fledged union, able to act independently before the law, could prove extremely awkward to the League clubs. Their very power over players was at stake. As Sutcliffe put it, it was now a struggle between the 'masters and the servants', and so the clubs decided to align themselves with the FA against the players and, in return, the FA declared an amnesty. The FA would overlook any misdemeanours that clubs and their officials might have committed. Thus, the fear that players might do as Meredith had done and turn 'King's evidence' was lifted.

As the *Athletic News* of 15 March 1909 reported: 'Until a week ago, the clubs, the employers, were under the thumb of the players and the union was quiet. But the FA offered a free pardon to the clubs if they would refuse to be dictated to by the players, if they would refuse to pay players sums of money in violation of the rules. The clubs consented to be honest and started with a clean slate. The players lost their power and ceased to be the real masters and now they have to rest content with a miserable pittance of £4 a week all the year through, many free meals and perquisites during training, and three months' holiday every summer if they are not taken for a continental tour – miscalled a football tour. The plight of the football player is terrible.'

The union's reaction to these moves was closer to organised labour. The General Federation of Trades Unions was the chosen body and on 31 March, a few days before the England-Scotland match, PU secretary Broomfield went to London to confer with players chosen to represent England, and meet representatives of the GFTU. Speculation was rife that immediate strike action was planned and the England-Scotland match was to be the chosen event. Why else, it was asked, were the England players involved?

The next day, an official of the GFTU was interviewed: 'We all appreciate the hardships of the players and the effective support a body like the GFTU with its thousands behind it could give, but it would be suicidal for the great body of pro-footballers to strike at the fag end of the pro football season. In any case, there are only a few hundred of the big players in the PU. The body isn't affiliated to the GFTU but could, of course, soon come within its ranks for the purpose of fighting out the question.'

On the morning of the international, Broomfield appeared in the newspapers sitting in conference with GFTU officials and a statement was released to the effect that the GFTU had 'advised a cessation of hostilities'. Broomfield announced, 'The general public may therefore rest assured that the players selected will be in their places.'

But the PU and Broomfield had miscalculated. The England players – many of whom were decidedly cool towards the Union – went out of their way to refute any suggestions that they would have considered striking. Broomfield had overplayed his hand and the next day the League spokesman, C.E. Sutcliffe, was quick to strike. He wrote in the *Athletic News*: 'Before turning out, the English players, all professionals by the way, sent a message to the football world which was a direct slap at the unwarranted suggestion in some morning papers that the international was played at the grace and favour of the Players' Union. . . . Our players are loyal,' he concluded.

Meredith tried to play the incident down: 'Don't believe a word of the statements readers ... there is not an atom of truth in it ... the whole suggestion as to the strike was made by the London Press and there is no doubt it did the union harm.'

Nevertheless, the Union pressed blithely on. A week after the Cup Final, in April 1909, Meredith plus player representatives from six League clubs, drew up the following resolution: 'That the union become affiliated at once with the GFTU and that the following rule be inserted in the minutes of the PU: That if the management committee finds it necessary at any time to withdraw from their employment such members be paid the sum of one pound until they resume their occupation.'

The Players' Union then proceeded to take a club to court under the Workman's Compensation Act in pursuance of unpaid wages, claiming that, 'the FA had no rule dealing with the same. The FA had had enough. In April it declared that in each new contract to be signed by the players at the end of the season would be a clause effectively disowning the Players' Union and declaring specific loyalty to the FA and its rules. As Jimmy Catton commented, the signing-on

THE CONSPIRATORS;
OR THE GUY FAWKES OF THE FOOTBALL CHAMBER.

The Football Association and the Football League, who are to meet in Conference shortly on the subject of players' wages and bonuses, are promised a bombshell from the Players' Union.

process would be an act of loyalty just as much as the enlistment of a soldier. Not to sign the clause would mean banishment from the game. It was either give up the Union or give up football.

In mid-May, Broomfield and Mainman, Players' Union permanent officials, were formally suspended from taking part in football again. The rest of the Players' Union executive had already chosen to resign. As the summer break got underway, more professional players signed the contract clause. Only one club took a principled stand.

Charlie Roberts recalled in his memoirs the moment of decision: 'I wrote to all my fellow players and called a meeting to be held at the union offices. Now, the majority of the Manchester United players resided in Manchester at the time and those who didn't replied to me stating that they would stand by the decision we arrived at. The meet-

THE CUT DIRECT.

Broomfield (to Meredith): Pooh! Who wants the old frump to recognise us?

ing agreed unanimously to stick to the union, and risk whatever penalties might be inflicted by the FA. Scores of letters arrived at the union offices from players on holiday saying they would resign until September when they would rejoin. They would get their summer pay alright and I thought at the time that we would be justified in doing the same, considering how the FA had waited until the middle of the summer to do a thing they dare not have done in the playing season.

'But ultimately I decided to have no underhand work, and I openly told the FA that I refused to resign from the union. At the next meeting of the FA the whole of the Manchester United players were suspended. The meeting was held on a Saturday morning and I remember the day very well. I am a newsagent in Manchester and when the evening papers arrived that day the posters read something like this:

'The Whole of the English Cup Winners Suspended Sine Die!'

'Manchester United Without a Team!'

'I had a benefit due, with a guarantee of £500 at the time and if the above sentence was not removed I would lose that also, besides my wages, so it was quite a serious matter for me. The players of Manchester United were paid once a fortnight during the summer and usually a dozen or so of us turned up at the ground each alternate Friday to receive our wages. None of us had received any official intimation from the FA that we were suspended so we turned up for our wages as usual the Friday after the suspensions were published.

'We waited and waited for our manager but he did not appear that morning, and all we could get out of the office boy was, "There are no wages for you, as the FA have suspended you all". "Well, something will have to be done," said Sandy Turnbull, as he took a picture off the wall, and walked out of the office with it under his arm. The rest of the boys followed suit and looking-glasses, hairbrushes, and several other things were for sale a few minutes after at a little hostelry at the corner of the ground.

'I stayed behind a while with the office boy who was in a terrible state over the players taking things away and he was most anxious to get them back before the manager arrived. "Come along with me and I will get them back for you," I said, "It's only one of their little jokes." I soon recovered the lost property for him. But it was funny to see those players walking off the ground with the pictures etc under their arms.'

Meredith had been here before, of course, though under different circumstances – a member of a Cup-winning side suspended by the FA – and, once again, a great deal of money was at stake, in particular, as we have seen, for Charlie Roberts. But for Meredith, too, the loss of wages was particularly hard. In June the outfitting shop into which he had put almost all his savings and earnings had been damaged by fire. No longer able to continue trading, he and his partner Millward were facing writs and summonses from creditors. In late July, Millward and Meredith were declared bankrupt – Meredith was said to have assets of only £35. Even then, he was cheerfully noting in his newspaper column that it could have been worse.

He wrote: 'By the way, the English Cup might have had a bad time the other day. A fire broke out in the cellar of my shop and did a great amount of damage. Among the articles it did not touch was the case of the Cup. The trophy, as it happens, was not in the case at the time. I wonder what would have happened to me if by any chance the Cup had been destroyed?'

During the summer months, interest focused on the rebel United side. They met regularly along with one or two others and trained at Fallowfield where reporters interviewed them and took photographs.

'We are fighting for our bread and butter and we shall win it too if the Newcastle and other players will only stand by us,' said one of the Outcasts. The name Outcasts had occurred to Roberts on impulse: 'After training a day or two, a photographer came along to take a photo of us and we willingly obliged him. Whilst the boys were being arranged I obtained a piece of wood and wrote on it "The Outcasts Football Club 1909" and sat down with it in front of me to be photographed. The next day the photograph of the Outcasts FC (showing the board and all the players) had the front page of a newspaper much to our enjoyment and the disgust of several of our opponents.'

In the background, sporting a straw boater set at a jaunty angle, Meredith stood, a rebel among rebels: 'Meredith, who is as keen on his training as ever was the recipient of much 'chaffing' owing to the fact that he is a kind of freelance at present, not having re-signed for the club.'

Though the Manchester United men had refused to give up the union, they had signed separate contracts with the club for the coming season, should it commence. Meredith could not bring himself to do even that: 'My position is a puzzle. I have not signed on for Manchester United and, as I am no club's player, I suppose I am not suspended, as I am a free player. I have, of course, not resigned from the union and, of course, do not intend to do so.'

As the close season of 1909 advanced the Union – in the shape of secretary Herbert Broomfield – lobbied sympathetic political organisations, including the Labour Party whose leader, Arthur Henderson offered his services as mediator at one point. Broomfield cajoled and chivvied players not to give up hope, insisting that by standing firm

The famous Outcasts picture. Back row (l to r): J. Picken, W. Corbett, R. Holden, H. Burgess, J. Clough, W. Meredith, G. Boswell (PU assistant secretary). Front: G. Wall, A. Turnbull, C. Roberts, T. Coleman, R. Duckworth. All the players were with Manchester United except Coleman who was on Everton's books.

and refusing to restart the new season both the League and the FA would eventually have to come to terms with an organisation both now seemed intent on destroying.

And as the days ticked down and it became clear that returning players were not prepared to ditch the 'Outcasts' of Manchester United, the FA did indeed agree to meet the Union executive to talk things over. In late August, agreement was reached on Union recognition and questions related to legal cases, but an overall settlement foundered on Union demands that the Manchester United players receive their outstanding summer back-pay. In an astute turn-about, the FA then attempted to go over the heads of the official Union by calling a mass-meeting of all professionals (but excluding Union men) for 31 August, just a few days before the new season commenced.

The FA was attempting in true paternalistic fashion to woo the 'men' away from the 'trouble-makers' (Meredith being a notable absentee). At the Birmingham meeting, attended by some 200 or more professionals, Charles Clegg of the FA made a long, rambling speech during which he blamed the Union for all the trouble, insinuated that the FA could destroy anyone's career if it so wished and concluded by offering to fund a puppet Union controlled by the FA – one without links with the wider Union movement.

His speech, though receiving a polite enough cheer, made little impression on the assembled players, who proceeded to call for various injustices to be corrected, for the Manchester men to be reinstated and their summer pay refunded and for the union to be allowed to negotiate on their behalf. In fact, various Union men *were* present, Colin Veitch of Newcastle being the most prominent, and it

Charlie Roberts who thought of the name 'Outcasts' on impulse.

139

was he who seized the initiative and gave an undertaking that the absent Union men would abide by any agreement reached with the FA (and by implication, agree to abide by the FA's rules) just so long as the Union was allowed to remain independent and free to act on its members' behalf. The 'Outcasts' back-pay could be settled at a later date.

Whether Veitch had consulted Meredith, Broomfield and the rest of the Manchester players on tactics is not clear. One suspects that he had not. The Birmingham meeting was a chaotic, somewhat bizarre affair, cannily manipulated by FA officials who correctly guessed that the majority of men simply wanted to start the season on time. A declaration that promised much but committed no-one to anything in particular was hastily drawn up and everyone departed in a spirit of false optimism and 'fudge'. Veitch probably argued that he had simply salvaged what he could from a potentially disastrous situation. But the critical moment had passed: the possibility of halting the season, the only way in which the powers-that-be would ever be brought to the negotiating table, had gone and it would be difficult to bring matters to such a head again in the near future.

Herbert Broomfield immediately saw the underlying motive of the FA – that they would recognise the Players' Union, concede to its members the right to go to court under the Workman's Compensation Act, remove all suspensions, but only on condition that the union renounce all aspirations to trade union status and thus affiliation to the GFTU. Therefore, they were to renounce the right to strike.

Thus for Broomfield, architect of that supreme moment of truth, the 'victory' claimed by some was no victory at all. A day after the season commenced he wrote to a friend, 'Thank you very much for your congratulations. I scarcely know where I am today. I seem unable to breathe. I am not overjoyed, though everyone else seems satisfied ... because there is something sad about the whole business, to think that athletes should be so devoid of moral courage is not a pleasing thought and if you knew my experience the afternoon of the conference you would feel as I do.'

William Meredith, interviewed a day later in the *Clarion* newspaper, seemed equally adamant that no victory had been achieved. On being told by the reporter that the FA had recognised the Union, he replied: 'Yes, provided the players observe the rules and practice of the FA. What's the good of belonging to a Union if one fetters one's hands like that?'

Sam Hardy, writing in *Thomson's Weekly News*, was also unimpressed by what had been achieved: 'The conference at Birmingham is now ancient history. My anticipation that it would clear the air was rudely shattered. . . It must not,' he declared, 'be peace at any price.'

Colin Veitch, on the other hand, was full of hope. 'Peace With Honour' was the headline above his article in which he claimed that the Birmingham conference had brought a complete settlement one step nearer. 'Step, did I say? . . . A gigantic leap is more accurate in description of the space covered!'

Veitch's famous conciliatory nature, his determination to press on with negotiations confident that the FA had the best of intentions, would, however, be sorely tried.

Putting a brave face on things, the Manchester United team, wearing their new Players' Union arm-bands, ran out for their first match to resounding cheers. Within a month, the arm-bands would be prohibited by the League. Their back-wages would take almost six months to be paid; Charlie Roberts's benefit match against Newcastle would be refused; and it would take the intervention of both Veitch and Broomfield to persuade the United men not to go back on strike.

As the weeks passed into months, even with Colin Veitch taking a leading role in the discussions, the elusive settlement seemed further off than ever. With no deadline set, no ultimatum, the football authorities felt free to linger, to prevaricate, to change their grounds.

By October Veitch was reporting back to the Union Management Committee that everything was back to square one. Meetings were useless with the FA insisting on their primary demand that the Union disaffiliate from the GFTU. Affiliation meant accepting that football was an industry and that players were workmen. It was a giant leap that the FA were not prepared to make.

With relentless, unremitting determination, League and FA administrators via their various newspaper columns and articles, kept up the psychological pressure: strikes would disrupt forward planning in football; signing a contract implied a moral duty not to strike; the FA could sort out all the game's problems, etc. The simple fact that the law of the land guaranteed any man or woman the right to strike, whether affiliated to the GFTU or the TUC, for that matter, made no

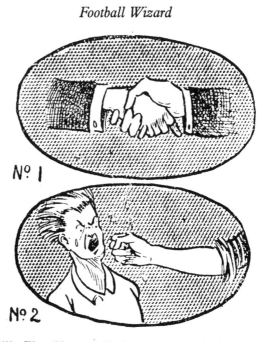

(1) The Players' Union badge as it is.
(2) The badge as it appears to some people.

Reader's cartoon.

difference. The FA was seeking a declaration of principle from the players; an acknowledgement that they were different, that football was a special world governed by men possessing ancient and benevolent wisdom.

There were many prominent players who agreed with all this, of course: Bob Crompton, Ernest Needham, William Dunlop – English internationals and influential captains who had played a part in the Birmingham conference and who were against 'unionism'.

And finally, in mid-October, the Union relented. It agreed to hold a ballot of all members to decide whether to remain affiliated to the GFTU. The vote was decisively against: 470-172. The Union thus passed a resolution thanking the GFTU for all its help. The FA lifted its 'suspension' of the Manchester players and paid them their money.

Charlie Roberts, however, declared himself disgusted with the result:

As far as I am concerned, I would have seen the FA in Jericho before I would have resigned membership of that body, because

142

it was our strength and right arm, but I was only one member of the Players' Union. To the shame of the majority they voted the only power they had away from themselves and the FA knew it.

Meredith attempted to put a brave face on things and even claimed a moral victory: 'The FA will be jolly glad they did not succeed in smashing the union to smithereens' he commented, adding that many of the players had 'voted under the influence of fear'.

But the settlement had been a great disappointment all the same. Early in November, Meredith at last re-signed, the last player to do so, the season already having started without him.

'I confess that the bulk of the players have not shown much pluck in the matter,' he said, 'but the clubs who have led the players forward and who voted solidly in favour of remaining within the Federation have the satisfaction of knowing that they behaved like men. The unfortunate thing is that so many players refuse to take things seriously but are content to live a kind of schoolboy life and to do just what they are told . . . instead of thinking and acting for himself and his class. . . A man said to me the other day, "Ah, the players have not the pluck of the miners," and he was right of course.'

For Herbert Broomfield it was the final straw. In December he tendered his resignation; anxious as he was to turn his full attention to his business, he would remain close to the Union for some time and even resume the secretaryship for a period in 1913 when the position fell vacant.

Meredith, as usual, was fulsome in his praise:

Herbert Broomfield is the first player who has pointed out to the players that they can protect themselves by unity and that if their cause was right they had no reason to fear saying so. He faced the power of the FA fearlessly, endured insult and abuse from his critics, worked night and day, travelled thousands of miles and spent at least £200 of his money because he would not touch Union funds until he had the consent of members to do so. . . How many men would have dropped into the background as Broomfield has done, allowing others more popular with the FA than he is to voice his views in order that his presence should not hinder a settlement? Very few, I think. A grander, pluckier fight was never made than Broomfield has made!

It would be another fifty years or more before the 'dreams of the visionaries' (freedom of contract, unlimited wages and bonuses, a percentage of transfer fees) would be realised. Whether Meredith would have approved of the present position of top players is debateable. As we have seen, he was all for top players earning top wages and a super-League would have suited his ideas concerning excellence and its inevitable rewards. But there is a contradiction here.

One of his constant themes, reiterated *ad nauseam* was that players ought not to be full-time, that men ought to have a 'proper' job to go to during the week and play football as a pursuit rather than a career. If that appears to run counter to the demands and spirit of his Players' Union he would probably have agreed, but might have gone on to point out that if players are to be forced to be full-timers, then they must be as free as any other workmen to earn as much as they can, to organise themselves as they see fit.

Meredith had been forced by Manchester City to give up his job at Black Park Colliery when he had been perfectly happy travelling to and fro between Chirk and Ardwick. He was quite serious when he claimed that a player could keep as fit as was necessary playing one or two games a week and training in the evenings. He was never convinced that weekend training camps were of much use and had seen scores of young men with acres of free-time on their hands squander their money and their talents on drink and gambling. Thus, when he demanded complete financial and organisational freedom for professional players he was pursuing someone else's ideas to their logical conclusion. Men must have dignity whether they be footballers or miners. To live as 'pampered idols' reduced many men to a pitiful state of dependence, no matter how brilliant they were on the field of play. Thus his Primitive Methodist upbringing, his parents' disapproval of the idea of playing a game for a living, can be seen to have left an indelible impression on Billy Meredith.

Why then, it could be asked, if he found professional football so difficult to come to terms with did he not stay an amateur? Many of his contemporaries did, including some famous Welsh internationals like Roose and Blew who played for top League clubs.

However, for Meredith, mining could never have offered the security that a profession like architecture gave to S.B. Ashworth, a member of the Manchester City Cup winning side. Had Meredith

THE KICK OFF!

The football season opened yesterday with every prospect of the dispute being finally settled.

been allowed to stay on at Black Park, he might have become a mining engineer, of sorts, but that was not to be.

More important, Meredith was obsessed by football and had ambitions to win international caps and trophies and play with the very best. He knew he had a great talent – and had to go to England if he wanted to develop it. Thus, it was not money alone that induced Meredith to turn professional. It was the game itself that impelled him to plunge into the turmoil of League football. 'My heart was always full of it' he wrote, and we must believe him.

The 'strike' of 1909 was a brave but confused affair. There was no crock of gold for players to inherit as Broomfield suggested (the mythical 'millions' made out of the game by directors and shareholders). What's more, professional footballers made up only a fraction of those playing the game up and down the country and thus the FA, the

MEREDITH OF THE TOOTHPICK

We wonder if, given the chance, the great Meredith would sacrifice his toothpick or the Players' Union Badge? (Thompson's Weekly News Picture.)

supreme governing body, was not an 'obsolete battleship' as Meredith had called it. It had responsibilities far beyond the then narrow confines of the professional game, and its motives were often misunderstood. There were certain attitudes that had to be changed particularly on behalf of some of the 'old school tie' FA administrators, but new attitudes take time to evolve – the 'strike' only hardened them. The 'up-to-date Dreadnought' of the League, on the other hand, was probably far more devious and hypocritical than it appeared.

What had been achieved was the establishment of a new Players' Union that would continue to grow, albeit painfully slowly, until it could truthfully say that it represented all the players, something it never did in 1909.

In the following years, Meredith, though no longer to hold office in the PU, was to continue to be an enthusiastic propagandist for its cause and its activities – in particular the gala sports days the Players' Union held to raise funds He also led frequent attacks through his newspaper column in *Thomson's Weekly News* on the FA as when the latter banned the wearing of the Players' Union badge on the field: 'You all know what the badge is like. It means unity, fellow-feeling and sympathy on the field and off; in fact, everything that is desirable.' But the badge was banned.

All his life, the Players' Union would remain as dear to Billy Meredith as his beloved Wales. He has been its most colourful champion. Indeed, on one celebrated occasion he greeted John McKenna, that venerable football administrator with the words, 'You are the Father of the League; meet the Father of the Union!' McKenna, Meredith claimed, was not pleased by the remark.

7

Triumph with United

'Signs are not wanting that Meredith has preserved his popularity. Enthusiasts know when he becomes at liberty to play. Meredith has received letters from South Africa, China, and many parts of the world wishing him well in the future. Many of the communications are from soldiers on foreign service. But perhaps the most convincing proof that he has not been forgotten is a present from two boys who have sent him two packets of quill toothpicks with their kind regards and best wishes. This was not a mere triviality. Their hero has not yet been destroyed. The youngsters admire the player and they at least have no qualms in blotting out the past. Let us all blot it out from memory and believe that Meredith is a man who will not only obey the laws of the Association, whatever they may be, but will obey the duties of sportsmanship.'
Athletic News, 31 December 1906.

Billy Meredith's return from suspension in January 1907 caught the imagination of football fans up and down the country, but for Manchester United fans it was an occasion unparalleled in their club's short history.

The *Manchester Guardian* reported: 'When Roberts led out the United team with its famous recruits onto the field there was a scene of wonderful enthusiasm. A greater roar of cheering has probably never sounded over a football ground nor probably has a football ground ever been seen in a more remarkable animation. The vast motionless expanse of faces which stretched upward from the snow-heaped sides . . . became suddenly moved and transformed almost as

149

a sea under a hurricane, and one saw nothing but an amazing tumult of waving arms and handkerchiefs. . .'

Meredith obliged the crowd with a typical dash for the bye-line and a centre that Sandy Turnbull, who had also been bought from City, headed in. Meredith recalled: 'The crowd simply went mad and during the next few days I got so many letters and wires congratulating me upon my return that I had to reply to them through the sporting Press. . .'

Meredith's return heralded the first great era of Manchester football. Manchester City's success had been marred by the suspensions and the bribery scandal. The team had not been able to fulfil its true potential. Manchester United, despite the Players' Union trouble and the 'Outcasts', were to surpass the City's FA Cup triumph of 1904 and establish themselves as one of the great teams.

United had undoubtedly seized the lion's share of the spoils from City's enforced break-up. Apart from Meredith and his close partners Turnbull and Bannister, they had also signed Herbert Burgess in the teeth of City opposition. An England international and probably one of the finest full-backs of the decade, Burgess was as sought-after as Meredith. Of the numerous clubs interested, Everton seemed favourites to secure him as they were prepared to offer City a much-needed player as well as cash. But United, in the persons of their wily chief-scout Louis Rocca and manager Mangnall, out-manoeuvred everyone when City had put all their banned players on sale at a meeting arranged in the Queen's Hotel in Manchester.

City did not do too badly out of the sale. Bury paid £750 for McMahon and 'Tabby' Booth, Bolton bought reserve goalkeeper Edmondson for £250, while Tom Hynds travelled to Arsenal in an exchange deal. Sammy Frost eventually rejoined Millwall (and his prosperous chain of confectionery shops) while George Livingstone, no stranger to travel, went to Glasgow Rangers for a large fee.

City received no fee for Gillespie, however. By now, broad and heavy and not a little bitter after years of derision hurled at him from the terraces, he travelled further from Hyde Road than any of his colleagues. As a final gesture to the football authorities with whom he had clashed frequently throughout his career, he sailed for America disdaining to pay his fine and taking his football boots with him. For years afterwards reports of his footballing exploits in the Mid-West

"HERE WE ARE AGAIN."

MEREDITH.   TURNBULL.   BURGESS.   M'MAHON.   BOOTH.   EDMONDSON.

The suspension of the Manchester City players by the F.A. expired yesterday, and some of them are expected to turn out to play for United, Bury and Bolton.
Manchester Evening News, January 1907.

and Canada trickled back to the stadiums and dressing-rooms he had filled with his huge energy and good-natured clumsiness. A year after the break-up of the team, George Robey reassembled the old side to play the new City eleven in aid of charity; Gillespie was the only absentee. To add a final touch of unreality to the occasion, Robey took the big Scotsman's place and even managed to score a goal – Gillespie would have found the idea of being replaced by a popular comedian loaded with unintended irony.

So much was to happen over the next five years, so much success, acclaim and controversy, that it is inevitable that memoirs of the period written by players involved make life at the time sound almost too good to be true. The comradeship, the dedication, the fun and games . . . they highlight the good and gloss over the unpleasant. Such attitudes towards Edwardian England pervade many memoirs written in the immediate aftermath of World War One – the physical and psychological damage of the conflict was still fresh in the 1920s and 1930s, and 'before the war' must have seemed like a dream-world.

And yet the memoirs record an enthusiasm born of an independence that professional footballers in particular were to lose during the inter-war years, an independence primarily on the field of play. Managers and coaches gradually brought their influence to bear after the war, as changes in the laws of the game necessitated new defensive formations and tactics – witness the Huddersfield and Arsenal teams of Herbert Chapman. But beyond the field of play there was an independence of spirit, among top players especially, a belief in the possibilities professional football could offer a man. The argument concerning money was still an open one, and although Manchester City had been severely dealt with, the Players' Union that Meredith and his fellow players formed felt certain, along with many of the League clubs, that change was bound to come.

By the 1920s and 1930s, such optimism and open defiance had been replaced by a more modest, servile attitude by the players, an acceptance of their lot and an almost army-like regimentation. It was a less colourful world altogether, in which professional football became big business for some, but no more than a temporary, albeit comfortable, sinecure for the players.

Thus, though memoirs of Edwardian times may sometimes seem too good to be true, they must not be dismissed as mere fiction. For

Like a silent tableau, its meaning unclear, Manchester United players pose for a picture. Meredith (second from right in cap) holds the towel. Sandy Turnbull is immediately to his right. Charlie Roberts, bottom right, stares at the camera, as does Moger (bottom left)

Meredith, in particular, the successful United days were the summit, the complete fulfilment of all he had ever wished for since starting out from Chirk some thirteen years before.

He was now a celebrity on a par with the music-hall greats of the day. Indeed, his fame had become material for some of the great comics, such as Fred Karno. A successful sketch of Karno's, called 'The Bailiff', launched the catch-phrase, 'Meredith, we're in!', that would endure for decades. It was once suggested that the comic had used the name to cash in on Meredith's notoriety (this was 1907, the year of Meredith's return to football). Certainly the phrase was adopted by Meredith fans, who shouted it whenever their man received the ball and set off towards the waiting full-back. The Karno sketch that followed 'The Bailiff' certainly seemed designed to exploit football's great popularity – and Meredith's notoriety in particular. This was the 'Football Match', starring Harry Weldon, a great fan and good friend of Meredith's ever since the City days. Weldon played a character called Stiffy the Goalkeeper, and the plot concerned a dubious character (played by Charlie Chaplin just prior to the latter's departure for America and the film world) who attempts to bribe Stiffy. Art imitates life. Karno exploited the connection even further by having famous footballers, Meredith among them, appear on stage poking their heads through holes in the scenery to represent the crowd.

The greatest of the music-hall comedians, George Robey, was a keen football fan and had been directly involved in the game throughout his music-hall career. He had played for Millwall and enjoyed nothing better than appearing alongside top soccer players in the many charity matches he organised up and down the country. Robey had lavishly entertained the City players during their successful Cup run, and he supplied the United players with colourful shirts for their Cup Final appearance, feted them after the match, and held fund-raising concerts for the Players' Union at the height of the struggle.

It cannot be said that Meredith took naturally to such a glamorous role. He was never at ease with the spoken word, never good at making speeches, invariably mumbling his words. The true nature of his celebrity was to be found in his cartoon image, his newspaper articles and, ultimately, down on the field of play where he was able to command vaster audiences than Robey. But he certainly enjoyed the

153

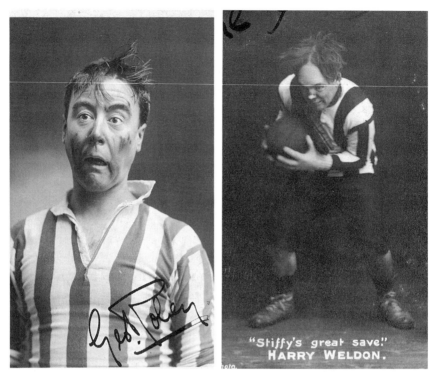

George Robey (left) had a genuine love of football, particularly the Manchester teams. He supported the Players' Union and was a good friend of Meredith's. Harry Weldon (right) played the part of 'Stiffy the Goalkeeper' in a Fred Karno sketch. He too was Meredith's firm friend.

acclaim and the fame. He was, above all, an accomplished showman, and the cartoon depicting him popping up through a stage trapdoor on his return from suspension in 1907 was more than apt.

The stage, setting and supporting characters supplied by Manchester United in 1907 bore an uncanny similarity to the City of 1903. United had only recently been rescued from financial ruin by a wealthy businessman and brewer, J.H. Davies, who was pouring a great deal of his own money into the club. They were managed by Ernest Mangnall who, like Tom Maley, possessed the knack of signing the right players at the right time. The club was newly promoted and full of ambition, and already possessed players in key positions who were of international class.

In particular, United had, in Charlie Roberts, Dick Duckworth and Alec Bell, a half-back line that would go down in football history as one of the finest and most influential of its era.

Along with Turnbull, United had also signed Jimmy Bannister and Herbert Burgess from City and a season later they would sign George Livingstone. Manchester City's misfortune had certainly provided a windfall for United. By signing almost a whole new forward line, the United manager had solved a pressing problem.

The *Bolton Football Field* said: 'There can be no doubt that Meredith's advent in Manchester United's forward line has worked wonders in the general effectiveness thereof for, prior to his coming, the Clayton club were woefully weak in attack, being frequently at sixes and sevens with the result that the management were often at their wits' end as to which line of attack to adopt and in fact no especial line was adhered to for very long, so disappointing were the results. Now, however, all this has altered and despite the occasional weakness in United's inside trio, the line as a whole, of late, has given extreme satisfaction. A good deal of this must be attributed to the prescience and power of the remarkably well-preserved Meredith who shows no decrease in ability. In his particular way, getting the maximum of results from the minimum of effort, Meredith undeniably is the greatest forward of all time and he looks like going on for a long time yet in first-class football.'

Despite the fact that he was by now thirty-four, Meredith still remained remarkably free from injury. Throughout the 1907-8 championship season, he missed not one League match, while some of his younger colleagues suffered lengthy spells out of the game. On and on Meredith played and the longer he played, the more refined his technique, the more effective his contribution to each game became. Said the *Athletic News*: 'The ball is glued to his feet as of yore and he centres square off the goal-line with everyone on-side. No wing-forward I know has the same elusive knack of slipping a back as Meredith. A back expects the flying Welshman to travel one way and finds himself left in the rear by a rapid veering circle made in just the opposite direction.'

The only thing that had changed since his City days was his ability to score goals prolifically. The goals still came but increasingly he confined his activities wide out on the wing, setting up the devastation that forwards like Turnbull and later Harold Halse were to wreak in the goal-mouth.

Training ground capers.

At the start of the 1907-8 season, Mangnall had bought a centre-forward called Jimmy Turnbull (dubbed 'Trunky') who resembled Billy Gillespie – forcing and bustling. The two Turnbulls, plus Bannister and Meredith, were the City forward line of old – and just as successful. With half the season gone, and nineteen games played, they were running away with the First Division title. Their record read:

Won 16   Drawn 1   Lost 2   Goals For 52   Goals Against 24

Jimmy Catton took a trip to Clayton to see for himself what it was that made the United team such an irresistible force. The principal feature, he felt, was the close passing along the ground: 'Over and over again I have bemoaned the practice of modern players in trying aerial football. The United delighted me by passing all along the ground. The ball was always rolling along as in a game of bowls – and from man to man in the same side. . . This is the puzzle of scientific football. The United provide an object lesson to every team by so faithfully and artistically manoeuvring on the grass. Even the centre was

156

COMING EVENTS CAST THEIR SHADOWS BEFORE.

on the ground, and therefore the easier for shooting, my dears, say these crafty men. . .'

The second important feature was the role of the three half-backs who pushed up in close support of the five forwards: 'If the United forwards couldn't play with the half-backs gliding the ball to their toes they would deserve to be drummed out of the game. If the ball was hollow wicker-work with a bell inside, five blind forwards could lead an attack with the intermediate line to set them on their way with a merry tink. Moreover the half-backs with the winged feet and the cunning toes play close up to their five forwards in the Corinthian style – and trust, as the Corinthians do, to the pace of their backs.'

Catton was a particular admirer of Charlie Roberts and the United half-back line in general, but he fully appreciated the debt they owed to the full-backs behind them, the third important factor in United's tactical success: 'And those backs have the facility of keeping the ball low. They never practice ballooning and their skimming drives remind me of the rule which was once in vogue at Winchester School – if not now – that no kick must be above shoulder high.'

The speed of interception by the full-backs and their accurate distribution was crucial to the success of the whole operation.

Overall, Catton considered United 'a team with a style and a purpose and not a collection of brilliant individuals with individual methods and a selfish diversity of objects. They were a United side in every sense, with a unanimity of style and a complete abandonment of the old wing-rush, lob the ball into the goal and trust to Providence.'

Billy Meredith sent this message to wife Ellen during a visit to Porstmouth with the United team.

Part of the secret of Manchester United's sudden success, however, lay off the field. Many of the United players were close friends. They all lived in the same district of Manchester and thus could have regular get-togethers at one another's houses, Meredith's in particular. He now lived in Longsight, in a house provided for him by Davies, and on match-day evenings the house was filled with footballers. Opposition as well as home players crowded in there.

Many of the United men had small businesses. Charlie Roberts had a tobacconists that later grew into a chain of shops and, later still, into a wholesale firm that flourishes in Manchester today; Jimmy Bannister was a publican – a trade Meredith would one day follow; Meredith himself had the outfitting shop; and Jimmy Turnbull was to become a prosperous money-lender. Thus, they discussed football, business and politics and, out of this close-knit fraternity, the new Players' Union was to arise.

Football, however, was the obvious subject and Meredith claimed that the United team developed many of their tactical ploys over the hot-pot suppers which his wife Ellen served up: 'We talked football and discussed fresh stunts to get the other fellows guessing. And then when we had decided that the unorthodox method was practical we went out upon the field and practised the movement with the result that in the midst of the match the new move took our opponents and spectators by surprise and often gave us a useful victory.'

Football correspondents were fascinated by these manoeuvres. The *Topical Times* commented: 'With head, arms and hands Meredith would make all kinds of quaint signals and a Manchester United player would be seen taking up a fresh position upon the field. Sure as death, in a few minutes the Welsh wizard would be seen chasing down the field and at the finish whiz! would come the ball within an inch of the player who had evidently got his instructions by the tick-tack method.'

The attempts to stop Meredith by fair means or foul, of course, intensified. It was forever being reported that he had been bowled over into the advertising hoardings, that he had swallowed his quill tooth-pick, that two, sometimes three men were constantly on hand to dispossess him or floor him: 'A roar of excitement such as set the nerves tingling greeted the first movement in the gigantic struggle and when Goldie checked Meredith, the London crowd simply

Meredith was brought down after-
shooting into Lawrence's hands

Meredith's
attempt was
sent behind by Dudley.

MEREDITH GETS DOWN
JUST TOO LATE.

LIVINGSTONE AND MEREDITH SHOW SOME
BEAUTIFUL COMBINATION

shrieked with delight. . .

'Meredith is a sort of Goliath in the eyes of football enthusiasts. Fulham supporters believed that if Goldie and Lindsay could suppress the Welshman they had half won the battle. And perhaps they were not very much wide of the mark. Goldie is a sleuth-hound and throughout the game he was ever at the heels of the United wing-man who, however, was not entirely eclipsed. Meredith once or twice tried to shake off the pugnacious Goldie who several times brought his arms into illegal service. In fact, I think Mr Kirkham was rather lenient in permitting these tactics to continue.'

Meredith was inclined to agree with the last sentence. It fitted his firm conviction that 'authority' was determined to halt him, somehow or other. It also suited his newspaper articles – their tone usually being combative and controversial. On the subject of his rough treatment, he wrote: 'I sometimes wonder why on earth referees don't speak to players who make attempts to catch me on the knees and ankles. They seem to think I am a special sort of person who ought to be fouled. Once recently a player kicked me in the knee and I asked

Action from the 1908 Charity Shield match between Manchester United and QPR at Stamford Bridge.

161

MAROONED.

William Meredith, Manchester United's famous International having been suspended by the Football Association was cut-off from todays Cup-tie between United and Everton.
Manchester Evening News, 18 January 1909.

the official in charge of the match if he didn't think it was a case of dangerous play and the answer was "no".'

But stopping Meredith was no longer the key to stopping the team he was playing for. Manchester United took the League title in 1908 along with the Manchester Cup and the first-ever Charity Shield. After a summer tour of the Continent, memorable only for a riot that occurred in Budapest when the United players were stoned by irate local fans, they started the 1908-9 season as favourites to retain the title. Injuries to many of their key players were to thwart that particular ambition but they gained ample compensation in the FA Cup. At the outset of the competition, however, in January, Meredith was ordered off against Brighton.

The *Umpire* reported: 'When there was only five minutes to play and the ball was on the right-wing Stewart and Meredith came into collision and Meredith was seen to lift up his boot and kick the Brighton player who fell to the ground. The referee at once ordered Meredith to leave the game, but he didn't seem inclined to do so, while the Brighton players swarmed around the referee to allow the great player to remain. But Meredith had to go, though he stayed on the touchline for a few seconds watching what went on. Immediately after play was resumed, Stewart came across the path of James Turnbull and the Brighton back had to be carried off to the dressing room and the match soon after ended.'

By the time Meredith returned from suspension, United had progressed to the quarter-finals, having dismissed Everton and Blackburn Rovers.

Burnley were their next victims (now captained by Alec Leake) and in the semi-final they were drawn against Newcastle United.

Just as when Manchester City had reached the Final by beating Sheffield Wednesday, their close rivals for the League championship, now Manchester United were faced with the team destined to take the title.

Newcastle were as strongly pro-union as Manchester United and there was quite a sense of brotherly solidarity about the occasion – the players cheered each other as they left the ground after the match and much was made by Meredith in his newspaper column of the sportsmanlike behaviour of the players on the field of play. They saw themselves as the cream of their profession with a duty to set the highest of examples. Nevertheless, the dictates of a Cup semi-final saw to it that it was an unspectacular game.

Meredith had been confident of his own fitness before the match: 'Personally I am satisfied that I am playing as well as I did last season when I was in better form than I have ever been in my life. The thing that pleased me is that I still have my speed.'

But Bramall Lane sported a surface of rolled mud and Meredith was a peripheral figure in a dour, unspectacular match decided by a goal snatched by Halse, an expensive signing from Southend and Meredith's new partner at inside-right.

And thus they proceeded to the Cup Final itself, truly the zenith of Manchester United's 'high Edwardian summer', a period when their fame as footballers was equalled, but never eclipsed by their infamy as 'Strikers' and 'Outcasts' as they had romantically dubbed themselves – men challenging football's establishment and, thus, as they were represented at times, traitors to King and Country.

The controversy surrounding the 1909 England-Scotland interna-

Enthroned at Last!

Newspaper Reader's cartoon April 1908.

tional had made it clear that the issue at stake as far as football's estab-lishment was concerned was loyalty – loyalty to the FA and thus to King and Country. Simplistic, but effective, and many players saw nothing ludicrous in the connection.

Someone had asked Billy Wedlock if he intended to play for England. He had turned abruptly and, with withering scorn in his voice, had said, 'I am chosen, am I not?'

And after the match, after the cheers for the King, one of the play-ers declared, 'The suggestion that we should throw over England is an insult to me and my father!'

The Manchester United players were thus to be distinguished from men like Billy Wedlock and Ernest Needham – stalwart Englishmen who spurned what they saw as the tyrannical pressures put upon them to strike and act like Bolsheviks.

The truth was that such a clear-cut division between union and non-union teams did not exist. Caricature and stereotype satisfied the Press and certain establishment figures – it made everything easier to handle. But, true or not, Manchester United would always be the glamorous 'rebels' and it must have been galling indeed to their enemies in the FA Council that the trouble-makers were so often in the limelight, lifting the glittering trophies and gathering so much popular support. The city of Manchester must have seemed a many-headed hydra – Manchester City had been chopped down, only for Manchester United to rise up in its place, twice as strong and success-ful, twice as popular.

Manchester United's opponents in the Cup Final of 1909 were Bristol City, captained by the same Wedlock, England captain, and the football establishment's favourite son – at least according to Manchester folk who always insisted that Charlie Roberts was a finer centre-half, but was 'politically' unpopular. For them and the rest of the football world, here was an opportunity to compare the two men's merits.

The *Athletic News* painted the scene: 'Wedlock walked on his team habited in royal blue, while Charlie Roberts ran on to the arena at a merry trot and very prettily the United looked in white jerseys trimmed with red and the rose of Lancashire on the breast. George Robey, who had presented the livery to United, was then busy talking to W.G. Grace, while Lord Charles Beresford, who was to present the Cup, had just taken his seat in the midst of a pavilion filled with distinguished visitors from all parts – even from as far as Amsterdam and Paris.'

But it was to be yet another Cup Final that failed to live up to expectations. One goal, scored by Turnbull after Halse had hit the bar, divided the two teams. United lost a full-back through injury and defended for most of the second half. They enjoyed a series of glaring misses by the Bristol forwards and Meredith almost scored on a lone raid before the whistle blew and Manchester United were the Cup holders. 'The game was a battle, not a brilliant exhibition,' Jimmy Catton concluded.

Meredith disagreed: 'These clever folk who have been twirling their moustaches and saying, "Aw, fearfully poor game, the Final, don't you know?" Really it is amazing. You can take it from me that the Final was not a poor game. It was a good game for dashing, keen,

Next Saturday the greatest football 'show' of the year will take place at the Crystal Palace –
The English Cup final, between Manchester United and Bristol City.
Manchester Evening News, 17 April 1909.

thrilling football, great goalkeeping and narrow escapes at either end.'

Perhaps he had been stung by remarks that he himself had achieved little in the game: 'Full of craft, Meredith danced along with the ball to the consternation of his foemen. He accomplished much in the style of the master but nothing came from all his efforts.'

The president of the FA, Lord Kinnaird, was ill and could not be present to hand over the Cup. A diplomatic illness, it was rumoured. By a strange twist of fate, the FA were to disown the very Cup itself a year later. The Manchester United players made a replica of it to present to Davies, their chairman, and the FA decided that graven images of their trophy were against the rules (though there was no rule to say so). The FA had another Cup made and gave the old one to Kinnaird as a retirement gift.

With the Cup won, however, Manchester United were presented

Meredith (far left) watches Sandy Turnbull's shot beat the Bristol City goalkeeper for the only goal of the 1909 FA Cup Final at the Crystal Palace.

with the keys of London by George Robey. The great showman, having dressed the team, now commandeered them and the Cup for a show he was appearing in that evening at the Pavilion Music Hall. Charlie Roberts recalled the chaotic evening: 'When I entered our dressing room there was the genial George all smiles and as happy as any of us. He asked me if I would take the team up to the Pavilion Music Hall, London, at nine o'clock, and take them on the stage as his guests and bring the Cup with me. I readily consented after all the kindness to us, and it was agreed that we would be at the Pavilion at nine o'clock.

'First we went to the Alhambra Music Hall where we were the guests of the management. I put the Cup in the strong room there before going to see part of the show. Sandy Turnbull, George Livingstone, Jimmy Bannister and myself subsequently made our way towards the Trocadero Restaurant where we had promised to meet some of our friends from Manchester. We found them there sure enough and the order of the evening was merry and bright. I forgot all about the time and my promise to George Robey until Sandy reminded me that it was a quarter to nine. Sandy and I jumped into a hansom and dashed off to the Alhambra for the Cup. We got it out of the strong room and were lifting it into a hansom when Mr Bentley saw us and said, "Where are you going with the Cup?" I told him of my promise to Robey and then he said, "I think that I had better come along with you two young gentlemen or I can see the Cup being lost in London and another sensation caused."

'With that he joined in. We took the Cup inside and of course left Mr Bentley to pay for the cab. Robey smiled when he saw us struggling in and asked me where all the rest of the team were, as he wanted us to stand for just a minute on the stage in view of the audience with the Cup on the table and, says he, "I'll be ready for you in about five minutes."

'I told him I couldn't possibly get the boys there in that time but that I had four players and officials with me.

' "Well," said Robey, "go and get somebody to make up the team," a request to which I soon complied. I went to the Trocadero which is right opposite the stage door and brought about a dozen of my friends from Manchester, including two or three men of aldermanic proportions. One had a bald head, and another had a silver plate in his side. Robey fixed us up round the table. I stood at one end and Sandy at the other while George Livingstone, Jimmy Bannister, Mr Bentley and Harry Stafford stood at the back, and with my friends all mixed in it was the greatest Cup team you ever saw.

'The cinematograph sheet was down in front of us and then, when we were ready, the notice went on the screen – "The Manchester United Football Team. English Cup Winners".

'The screen then went up and as the Lancashire folk began to cheer I thought I should have fainted and as the crowd were clamouring for a speech from me I was winking at Robey to get the screen down again

quick. He gave the desired signal and down it came and then the laugh that I had been bursting to let out came forth in its full strength. It simply was a scream to look at the team I had collected to represent the Cup winners! There was a poultry dealer, a publican, a mantle-maker, a bookmaker, a builder and a greengrocer among them and they enjoyed the experience a treat.'

Billy Meredith sat in the Alhambra where the game was being replayed on Bioscope. He and his wife Ellen sat in box seats, Meredith wearing a rather dowdy-looking suit. He had apparently refused to wear a wing-collar and starched front. The *Weekly News* noted the odd mixture the football folk made with the London Theatre audience: 'A strange mixture. Lounge suits and heavy boots sitting next to Mayfair dudes and smart ladies in decolette attire. Popular refrains were joined in by the trippers, much to the amusement of the audience.'

The next day, it was over to George Robey's house in Finchley where football stars mingled uneasily with music-hall artistes.

The *Manchester Evening Chronicle* reported: 'Wherever they go they say they are recognised and cheered in the streets. Cameramen snap-shot them at every turn, the unavoidable result of winning and wear-ing the laurels of fame . . . the men are looking forward to the home-coming. Several of them to whom I spoke today are tired of being lionised here. . .'

Back in Manchester, however, the celebrations continued. Following a League match against Arsenal, Roberts recalled, 'a torch-light procession was formed . . . from the ground to the Midland Hotel where a dinner was served, but I had slipped away from all that. I had had enough of the crowd to last me for a long time, and I was glad to get to my home and quiet.'

Meredith, too, had already retreated to his home in Longsight. A week later he and his family escaped to Chirk, taking the FA Cup with them.

But there would be no escape from the headlines and the limelight in 1909 as the Players' Union troubles continued. For Meredith there was the additional problem caused by the virtual destruction of his shop by fire in June. The bankruptcy hearing revealed the full extent of his financial plight. Though by no means a major partner, he had sunk all the money he had received from J.H. Davies on his transfer from City into the shop, plus substantial amounts paid by Davies at regular intervals. Among the creditors was Billy Lot Jones, a Chirk man who had stayed at City after the break-up and had reaped a bumper benefit the following season. Jones had lent the money to Meredith and his partner to develop a new and revolutionary football. The rights to the new ball had been assigned to none other than Herbert Broomfield, the Players' Union secretary, who now stood to benefit handsomely from anything up to £10,000. The money would have saved Meredith's business. As things stood, he had personal liabilities of £200 and assets of £30.

His financial plight explains, to some extent, his subsequent anxiety concerning his benefit match, scheduled to be played in 1912. He was now thirty-five years old and had nothing in a financial sense to show for all his years at the top of the profession. Fortunately, Manchester United were a rich club and J.H. Davies a generous man.

Fortunate too that Meredith's longevity as a player would continue to guarantee him a healthy regular income. Unlike many other fellow players, he had no trade to fall back on once football ended. He and his family had lived well ever since the late 1890s when City had reached the First Division. The wages which a trainer might receive, if he were to take such a course, could never match what he was earning as a player. Unfortunately, money was to become an obsession with Meredith, an obsession that would turn to bitterness as he grew older and rued opportunities missed, either through genuine misfortune, miscalculations or through punishments imposed upon him by football's authorities.

In 1919, he was to write: 'I have got the reputation of being somewhat of a disgruntled player because fate has caused me to "hold the dog" so often on behalf of my fellow players. And I have certainly lost a lot of money as a result of my fight for principle.'

But there was still a season or two of glory to follow as Manchester United continued to win trophies and as J.H. Davies continued to pour money into the club (an FA investigation into the club's affairs in 1910 revealed that he had paid over £7,000 in bonuses to United players over a period of five years).

His crowning glory, however, came early in 1910 when the new United ground at Old Trafford was opened. The last game at Clayton was played on 22 January when United saluted the past with a 5-0 defeat of Tottenham Hotspur. It was as well they were moving

Cartoonists loved Meredith's habit of chewing a toothpick as he made his way down the bumpy wings of Hyde Road and Clayton. In 1910, he was performing his party piece at the luxurious new ground at Old Trafford.

because, a few days later, the stands blew down in high winds. Old Trafford offered untold luxuries – games rooms, gymnasium, plunge bath for the players, and covered accommodation for 13,000 out of a capacity of 80,000. The grandstand offered tea rooms and tip-up seats – and attendants to politely point the way. The Pathe Film Company took the trouble to record it for posterity.

Manchester football seemed to have entered a new era and for Meredith the contrast between the old Hyde Road ground where he had first played in Manchester and the new Edwardian 'super-stadium' must have been a dramatic one. He had seen so much, achieved so much. Yet ambition still tugged at him; one particular mountain remained unclimbed.

Meredith's second decade in international football had seen the Welsh side making steady progress and two significant milestones had been passed. The first one had been Wales' first-ever victory over Scotland. Though Billy Meredith was still being forced to withdraw from international games this was one match he did not miss and he even scored a goal, his eighth in twenty-two games for his country. The win marked the end of Scotland's domination over Wales. In their next ten encounters Wales and Scotland would win three games apiece. Oddly enough, Wales' traditional superiority over the Irish was challenged during this period. Between 1901 and 1910 they won only one game, and in 1908, in the course of a 1-0 defeat at Aberdare, Meredith is said to have received some extremely rough treatment. He had already broken the crossbar, apparently with a fierce shot, when he was body-checked off the ball by McCartney who 'came swinging in swiftly and torpedoed Billy beautifully and sent him clean over the wire into the spectators.' Meredith, sprawling, swallowed his beloved toothpick. He sat up and looked vexed, saying to McCartney, 'Now Mack, no more of that – play the game.'

'Right Billy,' exclaimed the Irishman, 'but as you are a little too fast for me, I must bring you down to my speed.'

That same season had seen Meredith frustrated again, this time against England. Jimmy Catton recalls: 'The match between Wales and England in 1908 lingers in the memory for two reasons. First this was Evelyn Lintott's only game against Wales. I had a liking for Lintott both as a man when he was chairman of the Players' Union, and as a player for I first saw him in the jersey of QPR while he was an amateur, and knew him when he moved to Yorkshire.

'On this occasion at Wrexham, Evelyn Lintott had received instructions that he was not to give Meredith a yard of room, that he was never to leave him. I cannot imagine that this was the style of game which commended itself to such a sporting half-back as instead of a mere stumbling block he would sooner have met skill with skill.

'Nevertheless he carried out his orders so loyally and rigidly that Meredith could not move. In the second half when England had an overwhelming lead, Meredith turned upon Lintott and said, 'For God's sake, go away. England have got seven goals. How many more

WELSH INTERNATIONAL TEAM.

avies   J. Ll. Williams   E. Hughes   L. R. Roose   C. Morriss   W. Nunnerley   T. Kirkham
Chirk),   (Holywell).   (Tottenham Hotspur).   (Everton).   (Derby County).   (Sec.)   (Ref.)
h (Manchester City) M. Watkins (Sunderland) H. Blew (Wrexham)

Welsh team 1905. Back row (l to r): G.E. Davies (Chirk), J.L. Williams (Holywell), E. Hughes (Tottenham), L.R. Roose (Everton), C. Morris (Derby), W. Nunnerly (secretary), T. Kirkham (referee). Middle: W. Meredith (Manchester City), M. Watkins (Sunderland), H. Blew (Wrexham), A.G. Morris (Nottm Forest), A. Oliver (Bangor). Front: A. Davies (Middlesbrough), J. Hughes (Liverpool), G. Lathom (Liverpool).

do you want? Are you frightened of being beaten now?'

'The indignation of the wily Welshman amused Lintott but he never relaxed his grip until time had expired, and then he laughed at Meredith, who had not a smile in him.'

A season before, however, the second of the milestones had been passed – Wales had won their first Home International Championship. Meredith had missed the previous championship of 1906, suspended and in disgrace, and his frustration as Wales had beaten Scotland a second time, drawn with Ireland 4-4 and only just lost to England 1-0 must have been intense. Thus his return to international football in February 1907 in Belfast must have seemed like a rebirth.

The problem of obtaining the release of Welsh players from their clubs was as acute as ever – in fact, in none of the three championship matches that season did the Welsh FA manage to field the originally selected side. For instance, Charlie Morris of Derby County, and

Horace Blew of Wrexham missed two of the three games while men like Haydn Price, who was an occasional Aston Villa reserve, gained unexpected caps. The stalwarts like goalkeeper Roose, Morris of Liverpool, and Billy Meredith were obliged to give of their brilliant best. In the first match Ireland were beaten 3-2, Meredith scoring a rare international goal. At the Racecourse ground a week later, Scotland were beaten 1-0 by a Grenville Morris goal. Thus the match against England at Craven Cottage would decide the championship. For Wales, a draw would do, but Meredith was still seeking that elusive victory over the English and so he tore into the defence time after time in the first half until he eventually produced a centre that resulted in a goal. The ball seemed to run along the top of the cross-bar before falling to Evans to pass back to Lot Jones, who scored.

In the second half England equalised rather luckily and continued to live on their luck when a strong penalty claim for hands in the last minute was dismissed. Meredith never ceased to claim that victory had been snatched from their rightful grasp. But despite wholesale changes that had seen twenty-one different players used over the three games, Wales had become champions. A banquet was thrown and each of the twenty-one players received a gold medal. Welsh football had come of age.

The satisfaction at such a glorious return was more than compensation of the anguish Meredith had suffered, as he saw it, at the hands of the English. Yet Wales had failed to win against England, deprived of a penalty by an English referee!

The chopping and changing necessitated by the difficulty of releasing players from English clubs continued throughout the decade and Meredith was to have twelve partners at inside-right in twenty-two games. But Meredith could at least feel that the quality of various players in the Welsh selections was high. During the championship-winning year, he had played all three games alongside Billy Lot Jones, his Chirk compatriot and successor at Manchester City. Together they had scored three of the five goals that won the title.

But Meredith's most consistent partner throughout the first decade of the century was to be George Wynn, another Chirk and Manchester City man. Together they would turn out for Wales on twelve occasions. Wynn and Lot Jones were part of a select band of men who, along with Meredith, formed the backbone of the Welsh side from the

The Welsh side which drew 2-2 in Belfast in 1919-20 to set them on the road to their second home international championship. That season, Meredith (third player from the left, front row), at last realised his dream of beating England in an official international.

turn of the century. Charlie Morris from Chirk and Horace Blew from Wrexham, right and left back respectively, were partners on thirteen occasions: Leigh Richmond Roose earned twenty-four caps between 1900 and 1911, while M. Parry of Liverpool played sixteen times between 1901 and 1908, eleven times behind Meredith.

Blew and Roose were amateurs, but top-class players. Blew spent his career with Wrexham but Roose had spells with Stoke, Everton and Sunderland. Charlie Morris had a great career with Derby County, reaching the FA Cup Final in 1903 when he unfortunately had to deputise in goal. Parry spent most of his career with Liverpool and earned League championship medals in 1901 and 1906, playing alongside such men as Raisbeck and Hardy.

Altogether the six men – Jones, Morris, Blew, Roose, Parry and Wynn – earned 120 caps from 1899 onwards. Needless to say they were all from North Wales. In fact, it was almost entirely North Wales that won the international championship in 1907 and thirteen of the twenty-one players can be traced back to Denbighshire.

With Roose and Morris renowned as practical jokers, the Welsh matches were an entertaining, sometimes uproarious interlude in the hard, relentless League campaigns. If only the matches against England could have produced the longed-for win. Instead, in 1908, a year after the championship triumph, Wales were humiliated by the English, losing 7-1 at Wrexham. Jimmy Catton recorded this curious encounter with Meredith at Cardiff in 1910, after an international match against England. It had been a great day – Meredith had broken Billy Lewis' record of thirty-one appearances for Wales. But England had won 1-0: 'As we were wandering about the streets of Cardiff . . . he revealed a troubled soul, for he muttered, "I wish I had been born in England." This surprised me.

'He added, "You know the house where I was born was only three hundred yards or so over the border. What a time I should have had if I had been born an Englishman. I'm sick of being on the losing side."

'Then, after a silence, he burst out again, "Here, take my jersey", and he gave me the red jersey of wild Wales, in which he had played against England. I thanked him for the sporting treasure and stored it away at the bottom of my kit-bag as soon as possible in case he repented.

'More silence, until he said with dramatic eloquence: "I would like to be on the winning side for once against England. Mind you, we did win at Fulham in 1907 if the referee had given us our dues. But there, never mind, little Wales will win some day. May I be there at the death."

'The natural spirit was emerging from the black despair – and so to comfort him on the long journey before us I asked him to choose any briar pipe in the window of a tobacconist. The pipe soon restored peace to his soul.'

The Turnbull-Meredith Goal-scoring Syndicate did good business at Oldham last Saturday. They showed Oldham how to get goals.

8

Pre-war Days

'Every match reveals a want of proper understanding between Meredith and Halse. The immortal William is as clamorous as ever for the ball and so keen is he to be in touch with the leather, or is it rubber now? that one would imagine he hadn't seen a football for years. But that is no excuse for Halse sending it out to the touchline quite irrespective of whether Meredith can do anything with it or not. In response to Meredith's demands for the ball, Jimmy Bannister used to say that he'd give it to him when he could do something with it. Halse hardly goes on those lines. He mixes it a bit – Meredith getting the ball often when he, the greatest of them all, can do nothing with it and often failing to get the ball when the odds are tremendously in his favour.'
Manchester United FC programme, 29 October 1910.

Manchester United won the First Division championship for a second time in 1911. Manager Ernest Mangnall made some changes, replacing Jimmy Turnbull at centre-forward with Enoch 'Knocker' West and buying a new full-back and goalkeeper. Harold Halse was to have partnered Meredith at inside-right but the two men never achieved the instinctual understanding of other great Meredith partnerships. Halse was a talented goalscorer and very much a free-spirit, not one to settle down and act as hand-maiden to Billy Meredith. Thus he shared the inside-right position with someone more suited to Meredith's methods: 'Picken is a plodder and understands what Meredith requires. As jackal for the lion he provides well, but Meredith was to my mind the finest footballer on the field. His

Meredith and George Livingstone prepare for a training run on the beach.

mastery of the ball and his bursts of speed for short distance made him a frequent source of danger.'

Although thirty-seven years old, Meredith remained an important member of a forward line that included England winger George Wall, a speedy direct player with none of Meredith's, by now old-fashioned, ball-playing skills.

In the final match of the 1910-11 season, Manchester United had to win against Sunderland and hope that Aston Villa either lost or drew at Liverpool. Sunderland scored first and the small crowd at Old Trafford seemed resigned to defeat. Meredith then took a corner.

The Sunderland defenders gathered about Turnbull, who walked away from goal as if he had no interest in the proceedings. Meredith saw this and placed the ball just short of the goal for West to jump high and score with a perfect back-header.

Two more goals followed from Meredith centres and Manchester United had won 5-1. As they sat in the team bath a tremendous cheering rent the air and and they knew they were champions once again.

Another successful season followed, with Manchester United

HOW BILLY MEREDITH SPENDS THE CLOSE SEASON.

Thomson's News Photo.

Willie Meredith has gone to the home of his youth at Chirk for the summer. One of his favourite recreations is rabbit shooting. In our photo his little daughter Winnie is seen holding up one of the victims of her father's gun. Note also how the dog, " Don," is eyeing the rabbit.

managing fourth place, but the great team was now breaking up. At the end of 1911-12 Halse was bought by Aston Villa for £1,200 and manager Mangnall decided to cross the city and manage Manchester City.

For Billy Meredith, the much-discussed benefit match was approaching. In June 1912, it was announced that a working committee of volunteers had been established to co-ordinate activities. The whole of Manchester was to be canvassed for help and depots were established for the sale of tickets. Fittingly he had chosen the derby match with Manchester City.

Billy's wife, Ellen, with his two daughters, Lily (centre), and Winifred.

But it was not to be a purely Mancunian affair. Interest in the event was high across the UK and the Irish FA sent for a thousand tickets, while the Welsh FA established a 'shilling fund' and said they would donate the proceeds of two trial matches to Meredith's benefit. Three games for one man was unheard of. But Meredith was no ordinary man.

In terms of hard cash, however, the Welsh response was to be a poor one. In Manchester, on the other hand, smoking concerts were held to coincide with the big game and, as the day drew near, news of old City comrades began to appear in the newspapers: Charlie Williams, who had shared a benefit of £75 with Meredith in 1898, wrote from Brazil where he was training Rio Grande Del Sol, while Tom Hynds, the former City centre-half, sent his best wishes from British Colombia. And 'Tabby' Booth, an old City winger who was now working at Hyde Road, was helping to prepare for what was certain to be a record-breaking event.

On the day itself, there was almost a cup-tie atmosphere about the city, with supporters from Wales walking the deserted streets in the early morning. By two o'clock there were an estimated fifteen thousand waiting outside for the gates to open while in the main stand faces from Meredith's past were to be seen. There were former City directors John Chapman and Josh Parlby, the men who had brought him from Chirk; ex-Chirk players such as W. Owen, and Meredith's brothers Sam and Elias; and, of course, T.E. Thomas, Meredith's old schoolmaster. It was more than a benefit match; it was a celebration of one of football's finest careers.

Jimmy Catton was present, of course: 'There were celebrities in the seats of the mighty and humble folk on the spacious terraces but they all met to pay their tribute to a man of wonderful skill . . . In every clime where football is played either as recreation or as a sport that has to pay its way, the name of Meredith is just as much a household name as that of W.G. Grace. . .'

The club programme more than matched Catton's purple prose: 'The pen of the football commentator cannot do justice to the foot-balling genius of Meredith. Had he lived in earlier years he would have been the subject of an epic poem and been immortalised with Achilles, Roland and the Knights of the Round Table. This is a more prosaic age and we sit silent and watch with enthusiasm the weaver of

THEY'RE OUT FOR A RECORD.

The gentlemen in the picture are schemers for the establishment of the greatest football benefit of all time. William Meredith, the great Welshman, whose fame has spread to every country where "Soccer" is fostered, is to be the beneficiare, and no one will grudge another record to the man who has played in more international games than any other exponent living or dead. His committee, who have all figured long and prominently in the Manchester football firmament, are even at this comparatively early stage to be congratulated on the skill and energy they have displayed in the work of organisation. From left to right sitting are:—Mr J. Ayrton (Manchester City Director), Mr W. A. Tremlow and Mr J. P. Stephens, hon. joint secretaries; Mr H. Moores (chairman); "Billy" Meredith, the beneficiare; Mr Louis Rocca and Mr A. Leyland. Standing—Mr A. Hughes, Mr C. Schwarz, and Mr George Dale, who is busy organising a monstre concert to be held next Thursday in the Hen and Chickens, Oldham Street, with the idea of swelling the Meredith testimonial.

Meredith's Benefit Committee pictured in the Weekly News, *31 August 1912.*

football spells, this wizard whose feet are as fleet and whose heart is as buoyant as in that way back day in 1894 when he flashed into English football, destined to successfully challenge comparison with the greatest of outside rights that has gone before.'

In all, 39,911 people paid to watch Meredith's big game; £1,400 was the record total he was to receive. When he walked on to the pitch there was a terrific roar of cheering and cries of 'Good old Bill', the players heartily joining in the applause. When he went to toss for ends he had another great reception and the Irwell Prize Band played, "For He's a Jolly Good Fellow".

Afterwards, Meredith's satisfaction that at long last he had received his just reward was clear to all. A Manchester reporter wrote: 'For almost the first time in many years I saw William Meredith with a satisfied smile upon his face because he had at last achieved his ambition and atonement had been made for many grievous disappointments. Of a peculiar temperament, there has undoubtedly been reason for his lack of faith in mankind and things in general. After the FA

RIVAL "BILLS' SHAKE HANDS.

Billy Meredith and Bill Eadie, of Manchester, shaking hands prior to tossing for ends at the big local 'Derby'.

187

SOMETHING IN THE WIND.

Two Union stalwarts in Colin Veitch and Billy Meredith. The serious visage of the man of Wales would suggest that there are b reakers ahead.

Before a benefit match at Wrexham in 1912, Meredith (above) is pictured with the great Derby County and England star Steve Bloomer, and (below) shakes hands with his Welsh team mate, Charlie Morris, who was a member of the home international championship-winning squad of 1907.

Meredith and Turnbull were jointly responsible for the United's opening goal at Old Trafford, and the pair are here seen preparing to leave the goal, where Morley is seen gazing somewhat discomfitedly at the ball lying at the back of the net. The figure on the right is Emberton, the Notts half-back.
Weekly News, 9 November 1912.

stepped in and prevented his benefit at City ... he has always been doubtful as to whether he would enjoy the benefit that would make him safe from want in his later years. He haunted the directors' room at Manchester United until he got the date fixed, and it wasn't such an easy matter as some people might suppose and even then he was always of the opinion that something would happen to prevent the match being played, and I don't think he would have been really surprised if someone had told him that the FA had suspended the League and no more matches had been played. Perhaps now Meredith has discovered he has more friends than he thought he had, and that the world is not such a hard place after all.'

Perhaps, but unlikely. Within six months, Meredith and Manchester United were arguing about exactly how much he should be paid and exactly how much had been taken at the turnstiles. Incredibly, it would be another eight years before he would receive the full amount.

With the benefit over, the great days at Old Trafford seemed over too. Ernest Mangnall had now gone and no-one of equal calibre was employed to replace him. Charlie Roberts departed to Oldham and

Alec Bell to Blackburn Rovers. The club began to drift and the crew grew restless. Age was taking its toll where Meredith's form was concerned, and youth was waiting anxiously in the wings.

The Manchester United programme commented: 'If he would only introduce a little more variety into his methods and, in particular, loose the ball a little earlier, there is no reason why he shouldn't prove a thorn in the side of the latest English defences as he has been in that of former English teams. Now and again a natural perversity will tempt Meredith to play a style of game that leaves him open to be checked by defenders who are out to spoil sport rather than play the game themselves. Meredith can still hold his own with the best half-backs in the land, provided the latter will play the ball and endeavour to do more than send it into touch, but he naturally fails against defenders who resort to all manner of shabby tricks to prevent him from making progress. He could circumvent shady practices by parting with the ball quicker on receipt, but his reputation has been built on his amazing skill in beating his opponent while himself manipulating the ball, and small blame to him if he declines to join the ruck of players who wildly kick at the ball when it is crossed to them and trust to luck for it reaching one of their own side.'

The anxious youth in the wings was Sheldon who played a dozen or so first-team games during the 1912-13 season. For the first time in his career, Meredith was being dropped. He did not like it. He was said to be putting pressure on the management to play him; that he was trying to select the team himself. In December 1912, just three months after the benefit match, the United programme editor decided to clear the air: 'The club's position is clear. He (Meredith) was dropped after a series of unsatisfactory displays. Before this step was taken every resource of the club had been exhausted in providing him with a suitable partner. Others having failed to testify, Turnbull was selected. Here, surely, was a partner after Meredith's own heart! Not only is Turnbull the cleverest manipulator of the ball the game has known for a decade, but he happens to be a close friend of the Welshman. In his own sphere, Turnbull ranks equal to Meredith and the selection robbed the latter of any grumble he might have had of being inadequately partnered. The sequel revealed Meredith cold and unconvincing.'

The writer then touched on a more pertinent matter: 'One has the

Out of his shell again.

uneasy feeling that relations between the club and Meredith can hardly be the same as before. Everyone knows how thoroughly the directors tried to make a success of Meredith's benefit. He was allowed a perfectly free hand in arranging the match, and the ground was put at his disposal on the day of the match with City. Whatever he suggested was acted upon and the club moreover not only offered the services of players for the Wrexham match but also rested him on the Saturday preceding the match. How generous the United have been is shown by comparing the "gate" of £1,400 at Old Trafford with the treatment Meredith has received from his own countrymen who could not find it in their hearts to stump up more than £147 in two matches on Welsh soil. The position, as the writer sees it, is that the Manchester management has extinguished any indebtedness they showed to Meredith. Accounts were squared when he was permitted to reap a record benefit in football.'

Meredith pictured with another Manchester United player, Alec Downie, before Downie's Benefit game in 1908. Downie's match was a joint affair with Alec Bell, but even the presence of Meredith could not produce a bumper gate and the two men were said to be 'greatly upset'.

The following season, however, Sheldon was transferred to Liverpool, leaving Meredith in triumphant possession. Their paths were to cross once more, however, in unfortunate circumstances.

Manchester United drifted through the remaining three seasons prior to World War One with no-one to guide them and no talented youngsters to lift them. In 1914, Billy Meredith, turned forty, was now making headlines solely on account of his squabbles and arguments with both his club and the football authorities.

In 1914, the FA decided to collect a levy – a small tax on each professional footballer's wage – to make up a relief fund to support League clubs hit by falling attendances due to the drain of men entering the army. The Players' Union refused to co-operate as they had not been consulted and the clubs themselves seemed free to keep their gate receipts. Quite a number of professionals refused to pay the levy, but it was Manchester United who were singled out for the criticism. There had already been disputes between the players and the manager, the ageing caretaker J.J. Bentley. Indeed, the players were threatening to strike if Sandy Turnbull was not reinstated after having been suspended for arguing with Bentley in the dressing room.

The *Athletic News* wasted no time in attacking the players: 'We can understand their objections, which arise from an intense selfishness and an everlasting tradition at the club to be "agin the govnors". We have every sympathy with the directorate, who have always been afflicted with a body of men who have given more trouble than any set of players in the kingdom of football. It may be said that years ago Manchester United allowed their professionals to get the upper hand and that they reaped the whirlwind of their own folly. The mistake that they made brought their punishment, and has nothing to do with the present situation.

'Manchester United men were asked, in common with others, to give up a portion of their wages to go into a pool along with the levies on the gates of all clubs to enable their fellow players in other parts of the country to receive what is due to them. But it is evident that these men are without any feeling for their brothers on the field, and do not care a farthing about anybody but themselves.'

All of which was rather surprising considering that the United players referred to had been foremost in establishing a union precisely to support their 'brothers in the field', and that their insistence on

Meredith, in United colours, obliges the cameraman.

contracts being honoured was no more than what the League itself had demanded at the start of the season when some men had wanted to leave the game and join up.

The editors, however, continued to wipe the floor with the 'wretched men': 'Their interest in the game is bounded by what they themselves can make out of it . . . they are birds of prey . . . the people of Manchester now know the creatures they are supporting . . . so-called men!' And they concluded: 'They once called themselves "Outcasts". They deserve to be!'

Accusations of coercion and bullying were made against Meredith and Hunter, the club captain, and the two were suspended for 'insubordination'. It was reported: 'While the members of the team were waiting on the railway platform, they were asked what they were going to do. What was the answer of even the youngest player? "I shall have to go with the 'nuts' – what else can I do?" If this means anything at all it is that the leaders of the United exercise such powers over all the staff that men who wish to do what is right dare not. They are deprived of their free-will and action.' After much argument, fuelled in no small part by newspaper articles written by Meredith, the players fell into line and paid the levy.

More serious for the club, however, was a 'fixing' scandal that involved a betting ring and a prearranged result in a match with Liverpool. The match was played on Good Friday 1915, one of the last games to be played before the League suspended its activities until the end of the war. Manchester United had endured a bad season, and were in danger of relegation. They needed a win to stay up. They achieved their objective but the Old Trafford crowd booed and jeered them towards the end of the game and there had been rumours circulating Manchester for days that the game had been 'squared' or fixed. Later it was revealed that bookmakers up and down the country had paid out considerable sums of money to people who had correctly forecast the result, in particular, the score, 2-0.

In the subsequent FA inquiry 'Sandy' Turnbull, old friend and long-time partner of Meredith, plus three other Manchester United players, were suspended from the game for life. Among the four Liverpool players also suspended for life was J. Sheldon – Meredith's one-time apprentice. Centre-forward West later took Hulton Newspapers to court, charging them with libel and thus the whole affair was heard in open court, including an intriguing cross-examination of Billy Meredith.

Meredith's evidence suggested that he knew nothing of the arrangements made before the match. Anderson, Manchester United's centre-forward, felt otherwise. He was asked by Mr Cyril Atkinson KC, for the defence, 'Do you say Meredith was not playing fair?'

Anderson replied, 'I think that they all knew something about it before.'

Meredith denied the allegations. He said that before the match he knew nothing about it being squared but after they had been playing for a bit, he came to the conclusion that something was wrong. He made a statement to Beale, the goalkeeper. At half-time he was practically starved, and after the second goal he got no chance whatever.

He was asked, 'In your opinion, could anyone have played in that game without suspecting there was something wrong?'

'No.'

'Was there any reason for such play at a time like that?'

'No.'

'If you had got the ball were you perfectly fit and ready to go on and take advantage of it?'

'Quite.'

Replying to Mr Atkinson in cross-examination Meredith claimed that he played his hardest whenever he got the ball. He sent word up the line to the captain and at half-time he asked what was the reason for starving him. They said they were doing their best. Meredith said he didn't think so. He would not agree with counsel that play in the first half was exceptionally good.

'Because you were not getting your fair share of the play?'

'No, I have had plenty of the ball when it has been a poor game.'

He continued by asserting that what had gone on during the game was unjustified in terms of footballing strategy and that he had been disgusted with the whole affair.

After three days of futile argument, the judge ruled for the FA and Hulton Newspapers. The rules of natural justice, he decided, need not apply in cases decided upon by the FA, because the latter was a privileged institution, with a duty to prevent dishonesty in the game. As long as the FA acted without malice, then those bound to obey its rules – i.e. clubs and players – must accept its judgements whether they feel they have had a chance to defend themselves or not. The professional footballer, it seemed, was still outside the law; the FA was still his lord and master.

Meredith's part in this shabby business seems to have been a peripheral one. Perhaps he watched the furtive arrangements going on from the corner of the dressing room and simply turned a blind eye – he had seen it all before, and suffered the consequences. Perhaps he no longer cared what went on among his colleagues. There had been so much unpleasantness between the club and the players prior to this – the FA levy, the squabbles in the dressing room, the wrangles with the club over his benefit money still outstanding. Perhaps he was content to concentrate on his new public house, the Church Hotel. He was forty years-old; the majority of his playing colleagues were half his age.

Meredith never spoke again about the betting ring scandal; he would simply laugh, shift his toothpick from one side of his mouth to the other, and change the subject.

9

The Final Flourish

'Did you receive a letter with some things which a pal and I took from a lad who was lying in front of our trench? I have been wondering if you knew him and if his relations are about Clayton. It was a start to me when I turned the poor lad over and saw he belonged to that district of Manchester. It brought back memories of many a happy day. We buried him as decently as we could. I stuck a bit of wood with his name and number at the top of the grave.'
Sandy Turnbull in a letter to Charlie Roberts, 1916.

The Football League programme was suspended in 1915. Players were free to join up and go to France and hundreds did so. There was even a Footballer's Battalion formed as part of the Middlesex Regiment, although organised football at home continued on a regional basis. The War Leagues provided entertainment for an increasingly depressed and deprived population. Teams were allowed to sign on 'guest' players. If a professional from another club was on hand and willing to play, he could do so.

Sandy Turnbull, banned for life after the betting and bribery scandal, joined up in 1916. Some months after discovering the dead Manchester boy outside his trench, Turnbull himself was killed in an advance on enemy lines. So ended the life of one of the best Scottish inside forwards never to have played for his country. A colourful, if at times rather dubious character, his epitaph must remain those mock-

Sandy Turnbull had a dream that he would win the Players' Union sports by a mile. A news-paper set up a picture of the dream.

heroic lines written after the 1909 FA Cup Final, when he scored the only goal after almost missing the match through injury:

> *Why we thought you were 'crock'd', – Dashing Sandy*
> *That to Fame your road was block'd – Hard lines Sandy!*
> *But you came up to the scratch,*
> *Made an effort for THE match,*
> *A great victory to snatch – Bravo Sandy!*
> Athletic News, 24 April 1909.

In the same year that Turnbull left for France, back at Hyde Road where he and Meredith had started their successful careers, his old partner was donning the familiar blue shirt of Manchester City once again. The *Athletic News* reported: 'After an absence of close on eleven years, Meredith reappeared in the colours of Manchester City and though it was his first game of the season he could safely take credit to himself that he was unsurpassed by any other forward on the field. Naturally his pace has slackened and he didn't centre with the same facility as of yore. He couldn't lift the somewhat heavy ball, but his feet have not yet lost their cunning and there was none that can back-heel with such certainty as he.'

Manchester United and Meredith were still at loggerheads. United held the balance of Meredith's benefit money – their policy had been to dole it out in instalments, along with the interest – but now the club were demanding to see certain ticket receipts which Meredith could not supply. Old Trafford was no longer a happy place to be. The vast new ground had proved a financial burden to the club, they had still not replaced Mangnall, nor had they replaced key players. Manchester City, on the other hand, had rebuilt themselves since the 1906 disaster. Familiar faces like Josh Parlby and Lawrence Furniss were returning.

In 1915, Meredith took a Davies pub on Stockport Road, but as it was much closer to Hyde Road than Old Trafford, and with the general relaxation on registration of players due to the war, he applied to play again for City. It must have been like the prodigal's return: 'There is a particular spot on the Hyde Road ground which deserves to be known as "Meredith's patch". It is the place from where the famous Welshman has made history, and from where on Saturday in the match with Blackpool, he added to the long and glorious line of successes which he inaugurated twenty-two years ago. The master knows it to an inch, almost to the blade of grass, and the manner in which he crossed the ball from the old familiar spot and gave Barnes and Brennan the chances from which they won the match vividly recollects the halcyon days of his wonderful association with "Sandy" Turnbull.

'That profitable relationship has been broken, never, I fear, to be resumed, but Meredith goes on and on, playing though he was when the majority of his colleagues were at school. Not one amongst them had a greater part in the City's opening victory of the season than the still useful "Wizard of Wales".' *Athletic News*, 25 September 1916.

To men returning from the nightmares of France and Belgium, retracing their steps down to the Hyde Road for an afternoon's blessed normality, the sight of Meredith still prancing down the right wing must have seemed like a sweet dream.

The War Leagues were poor substitutes for the real thing. The standard of play gradually deteriorated as more and more men went to France and never returned, as more young, raw players were taken on to fill the gaps. With so many players 'guesting' for different clubs, there was little continuity and only older men who could not be expected to join the army retained their places from week to week. Three men played almost continuously throughout the three War League seasons for City: Eli Fletcher and goalkeeper Goodchild, both of whom had signed on in 1911, and Billy Meredith who had first appeared for City in 1894. Now in his mid-forties, Meredith had lost none of his appetite for the game despite the continuing efforts of defenders to knock him out of his stride. Though an increasingly successful publican, he always found the time to turn out for City, as well as in countless charity matches supporting a variety of causes. But battles with Manchester United still remained the most keenly contested of all games, Meredith usually managing to produce something unusual to match the occasion. Jimmy Catton, in March 1917, wrote this typical eulogy of his favourite player creating the winning goal yet again.

'Meredith skirted the touchline until he was almost level with the corner of the penalty zone. "Now or never" said a man with baited breath behind me. He was right. And it was Now. Meredith, with a comprehensive glance, saw the opportunity and knew the value of the fleeting seconds. Gathering himself, he made a brilliant centre. Perhaps it was a drive for goal. He alone can tell. In an oblique direction the ball travelled rather below the height of the crossbar. It seemed to be speeding straight for its destination – as truly as "black arrow" released from a yew bow by a deadly archer.

'John Mew, dark of hue, lithe of limb, strong and brave, had met and repelled many fierce attacks in the preceding stages. Once again he left his charge and advanced to the edge of the goal area. Many times he had done so and never failed. Why should he fail now? He sallied forth but the ball was just a little higher than he had estimated. With the tips of his fingers he just scraped the leather case but he could not stay the course of the drive. The ball passed behind him – Barnes nodded it in. . .

'In my days I have seen a few players, but no such artist as Meredith, defying time with his steady steps, and adversaries who count it an honour to checkmate him now when the fleetness of youth is supposed to have forsaken him. But has it?'

In October 1918, a few weeks before peace was restored, Meredith celebrated twenty-four years in first-class football and later that same season – the last of the War Leagues – he formed part of a forward-line that gave some glimpses of the good times ahead for City.

Horace Barnes, Tom Browell and Tom Johnson all figured in a series of high-scoring wins (twenty-three goals in six games), after one of which a reporter asked Billy Meredith if he really thought that, like Tennyson's brook, he could go on forever. But the only reply that question elicited was a characteristic tug at the nap of his cap and, 'I'm not done yet'.

Popular though he was, there must have been many who found the headlines in 1920 announcing that Meredith was in dispute with his club and refusing to sign on, depressingly familiar. The war over, Manchester United claimed him, but Meredith did not want to return.

It was the old problem of transfer fees: 'Today I am kicking my heels in idleness because Manchester United have the power to fix a fee upon my head for my transfer to any club desirous of my services. True they have offered me the maximum wage and consequently the authorities turned down my appeal for a free transfer.

'But I am no sentimentalist. I am quite prepared to play for Manchester United and accept the wages offered. But before I accept those terms, I believe I have the right to make other demands.

'I maintain that it is the blackest injustice to place a price upon the head of a player for whom they paid no transfer fee.'

The squabble over transfer fees led directly to the very nature of the professional game; though at times a little muddled, his arguments did have a certain consistency: 'Restrictions upon natural develop-ment only cause cunning brains to set to work to drive a coach and four through the laws. If a player becomes a star and his own club cannot or will not risk paying him more than the legal wage, in the past at any rate many clubs could be found to do so and the club has had to take a transfer fee in place of the player they probably would have preferred to keep.'

But his refusal to be transferred was essentially a personal repug-nance at being considered a piece of merchandise: 'I am still firmly of the opinion that the selling of players is a degrading business, and I have proved that, so far as I am concerned, I will not allow a price to be put upon my head. I would rather have ended my career as a footballer than allow any club to sell me even for a packet of Woodbines.'

United had offered him £10 a week plus £700 as settlement of the benefit arrears, but he was adamant: 'The paltry pittance is not magnetic; Achilles still sulks in his tent.'

But not entirely. Though spurning League football, Meredith was still eligible to play for Wales. In the Victory international against England in December 1919, he was made captain. He won the toss with a 'lucky' penny given him by Ted Robbins, Welsh FA secretary, and after twenty-two minutes he scored Wales' first goal. A free kick was swung out to the right and Meredith fastened on to the ball. With rare pace after all those years he took off with Grenyer in pursuit and Knight looking for the centre. Meredith centred – right into goal. Williamson bent down to gather the ball but to the amazement of everyone he allowed it to roll between his hands and legs into the net.

It was a poor game but Wales scored again and hung on to win 2-1. At the final whistle, amid deafening cheers, Meredith seized the ball and ran from the field. It seemed the fulfilment of his dearest wish, a win against England. 'Oh, that I have lived to see this day!' he told Catton in the dressing room. But it was merely a prelude.

The Victory internationals were unofficial – the results were not entered into the records and, though Meredith was perfectly happy to regard the Cardiff game as the pinnacle of his international career, greater things were in store. Six months later Wales were to beat England once again, only this time in a full international – a victory that would bring them their second championship.

After a 2-2 draw in Belfast, Wales met Scotland at Ninian Park and in front of sixteen thousand Welshmen they fought out another draw, 1-1. Meredith had a hand in the Welsh goal: a corner from Richards was fisted away by the Scottish goalkeeper Campbell. The ball went straight to Meredith who shot, it cannoned off a defender into the path of Jack Evans, whose shot went in off an upright.

A few weeks later Wales met England on a snow-covered Highbury pitch. It was to prove Billy Meredith's last appearance for his country, and a truly fitting climax to his long career. Richards and Davies scored the Welsh goals, and if Meredith's own part was less dramatic, he had achieved the victory he had dreamt of for almost thirty years. Afterwards, in the dressing room, they said that he wept unashamedly. He was entitled to his tears. It had, after all, been a long

The Welsh side which beat England 2-1 in a Victory international in October 1919. Back row (l to r): Billy Meredith, Fred Keenor, F.J. Peers, Charlie Matthews, Lloyd Davies, W. Goodwin. Front: Ted Hughes, Lot Jones, J.T. Jones, Stan Davies, Ted Vizard.

and difficult trail.

Selected for every international since 1895, he should have had sixty caps. Instead, it was forty-eight (though he claimed for years that it was fifty). In twenty full internationals against England, he had seen his gallant Welsh side lose fifteen times, conceding fifty-seven goals and scoring just fourteen in reply. Meredith himself had managed only two goals in all those years. If anything could be said to have been a David and Goliath struggle, this was it.

But Welsh soccer, both at club and international level, had now come of age. There would soon be six professional clubs from the Principality playing in the Football League, and in the south, Cardiff would challenge strongly for both League title and FA Cup.

The heyday of North Wales was over and Billy Meredith, their most illustrious representative and Wales' first great soccer player had now left the international stage. In 1922 he was presented by the Welsh FA with a silver epergne to commemorate his record number of caps.

Yet still Meredith did not retire from professional football. During the 1920-21 season he reluctantly played fourteen first-team games for Manchester United and although he never made more than three consecutive appearances, his inclusion in the team was always looked forward to. The spectators rejoiced when they saw his name on the blackboard announcing the alteration of the team. Meredith, to borrow a phrase from the racecourse, was a 'chalk jockey'.

In 1921, Manchester United finally relented and Meredith moved back to City on a free transfer. On 8 August, Meredith's picture appeared on the front page of the *Athletic News* above the caption, 'City's new player-coach'.

In 1923, the Hyde Road ground was closed. Manchester City were building a new ground to the west of Ardwick and Gorton, at Maine Road. Meredith had returned to play out the last of the Hyde Road days. For the first half of the 1921-2 season he held his place on the right wing, playing twenty-five games in all. At the end of October 1921 he appeared in the last 'derby' match to be held on the Hyde Road. City won 4-1 and the headlines next day declared: 'Barnes's Big Day. Wonderful Meredith!'

'The most skilful outside forward on the field, the man who showed the best ball-control and who passed and kicked with the best judgement all through the first half during which period the match was won and lost was William Meredith. . .

'Meredith came loping along the home right wing. When challenged he turned the ball back to Warner with one of those deft touches which are the inheritance of his long experience and natural ability. Warner did the right thing. He promptly drove the ball hard and low across the face of the goal. The rain had made the ground greasy. Barnes dashing up on the left wing, perhaps ten yards wide of the post caught the ball with his left instep as he fell and turned it swiftly just inside the post nearest to him. It was one of those goals which comes to a man once in a lifetime.' *Athletic News*, 24 October 1921.

On 5 May 1923, Meredith played his last game at Hyde Road, almost the last football match played on the old surface beneath the shadows of the railway arches – a reserve match against Preston North End. Wembley Stadium had just staged its first Cup Final. Maine Road would open the next season with a capacity of 76,000. It seemed unlikely that Meredith would step out on to the turf of either because at forty-nine he was well into middle-age and successfully running a public house. He was a Manchester personality officiating at charity matches and appearing on the silver screen. In 1924, he appeared in a 'short' called *Wireless Football* demonstrating his skills and giving a few hints on 'how it is done with the ball'. In the evenings he would appear on stage to answer questions sent up from the audience. The cinema was to continue to fascinate him just as the music-hall had done. In the 1930s he had shares in various small cinemas in Stretford.

At the Church Hotel, though never the epitome of 'mine host' as he hardly ever drank, never smoked and rarely served behind the bar, he enjoyed a popularity that made the hotel a thriving business. His name was prominently displayed outside (local people knew the pub simply as 'Meredith's') and his wife Ellen and members of the family

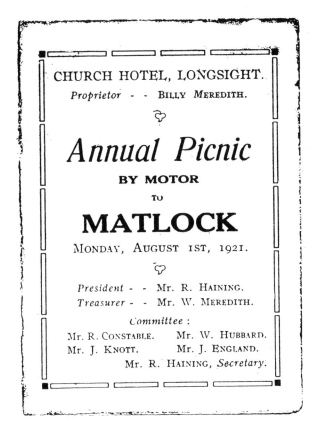

CHURCH HOTEL, LONGSIGHT.

Proprietor - - BILLY MEREDITH.

Annual Picnic

BY MOTOR

TO

MATLOCK

MONDAY, AUGUST 1ST, 1921.

President - - Mr. R. HAINING.
Treasurer - - Mr. W. MEREDITH.

Committee :

Mr. R. CONSTABLE.   Mr. W. HUBBARD.
Mr. J. KNOTT.   Mr. J. ENGLAND.
Mr. R. HAINING, Secretary.

from Chirk helped to run the place. There were usually sisters and aunts, cousins and nephews from Wales to be found there – but as well as being the focus of his family life, the Church Hotel was also a sporting centre. Famous sportsmen could be spotted standing at the bar chatting with Billy; journalists waited upon the great man for a controversial quote. Meredith was never averse to speaking his mind though he reserved most of his comments for his football columns in the sporting Press, where he tipped future champions and cast a caustic eye over his successors.

But though comparatively well-off during the 1920s and 1930s, he still refused to adopt the lifestyle appropriate to his status. Though his wife might send the two daughters out into the world, admonishing them – 'Be good. Everyone knows your father!' – Billy never seemed to care about what others were thinking, nor what was or what was not in vogue. After his trip to Europe with Manchester United in 1908, he had declared he would never travel abroad again, and he did not, turning down a coaching appointment in Budapest. Though his wife and daughters took holidays abroad, he stayed at home. And though the family eventually acquired a car, he never learned to drive it; someone else had to drive whenever he went anywhere in it. He preferred to walk whenever possible.

And though to the world at large and to newspaper reporters in particular he could appear terse and even rude, at home his true nature emerged. He was an elaborate practical joker, the days away on special training and with the Welsh team having given him a taste for pranks and leg-pulling. He let ponies loose in the barmaid's quarters; he bribed his young nephew with a penny to pop his head round the kitchen door and shout 'Bugger!' to scandalise his strait-laced maiden-sisters. He named his cat Bung and his terrier Blitz, and had a parrot that he taught a risque line in choice words; eventually his wife, unable to tolerate the bird any longer took it to Belle Vue without his knowledge and let it free. 'Where's that bloody parrot?' his young nephew remembered him saying for months afterwards. 'Come on Billy, get your coat,' he would say, and off they would go to Belle Vue in search of his parrot, or further still in search of some countryside.

But, settled though he may have appeared, Meredith never ceased his daily training routine. His coaching job at City was the excuse, but training had long been an obsession with him. He would go to the ground after everyone else had gone home, as he had done as a player, and practise corner-kicks and place-kicks while Billy his nephew fetched the ball for him up and down the terraces. At the Church Hotel he would set up crates in the Buffaloes meeting room and dribble round them using a tennis ball he always seemed to have in his pocket. He was still sparsely built, still the same weight he had been as a player – it had earned him in his later years the nickname 'Old Skin', which he disliked. But his physical condition continued to matter to him and though his old colleagues, many now gone to fat, might mock, he was to have the last laugh on them all. In 1924, Meredith's regular habits and meticulous routine were to pay off one last time.

In February, Manchester City were drawn against Brighton in the last sixteen of the FA Cup. Though a Third Division South club, Brighton had a good record for upsetting better teams – they had already knocked out Everton that season. The tie was to be played at the Goldstone Ground, and Manchester City could not be certain of proceeding to the quarter-finals. Manager Mangnall, Meredith's old boss at Manchester United and City manager since 1912, decided to take a gamble. On 24 February, the *Athletic News* announced: 'The city of Manchester took short breath and laughed in incredulous vein when it was announced that William Meredith was going to play for Manchester City against Brighton. People declared the directors were losing their judgement and courting defeat.'

Meredith had played only four full games that season – three Lancashire Cup-ties and a reserve game in December. He had not played a first-team game for more than a year. In July he would be fifty years old. Meredith himself was unconcerned. He packed his bag and on Friday night travelled down to join the team at Brighton.

Ivan Sharpe, Jimmy Catton's successor at the *Athletic News*, found the sudden interest in Meredith by the popular Press very amusing: 'Therefore, for the evening newspapers of that day in 1924, Billy Meredith becomes a news story. Therefore, a Fleet Street newsman as distinct from a sports correspondent goes on his trail. If he knows nothing of football, so much the better. He will keep off football topics – keep off the grass, so to say – and give the news editor what he wants. . . The human angle, and only the human angle, and if that old

Billy Meredith with Bulloch, Simpson, and Mee, three of the Manchester City players, into whom the Welsh wizard is busy instilling the complete art of football.

Weekly News, 14 January 1922.

schoolmaster can be raked up and taken to the match to watch his pupil play, that's fine, and we'll pay for the bath-chair. . .

'The newsman met Meredith at Brighton railway station, walked with him along the platform putting preliminary questions about his football to establish the intimate touch. The newsman asked him whether he had played a Cup-tie before, or in an international match and had he on any of these occasions ever scored a goal? Meredith was more patient than Bloomer but he, too, could be terse. Star and journalist parted company before they even reached the end of the plat form. The newsman hadn't got as far as the news editor's humanities. No story.'

The point, of course, was that Meredith was from another age. A new football generation had grown up knowing nothing of him other than his name and record. It had been fifteen years since he had played for Manchester United in the Cup Final of 1909. But there were many who did remember, and telegrams flooded into the dressing room at Brighton. One read, 'Congratulations, Billy, may you lift the Cup again. Snowball Frost.'

And supporters and journalists of a generation past were equally intrigued. 'Analyst' of the *Topical Times* spoke for many of them: 'When I heard that he was to be resurrected for the purposes of the third round against Brighton and Hove, I took myself to the match with every possible speed. And on my way to Brighton I found in the Pullman at least half-a-dozen friends who years before professed that they had lost their fondness for soccer.

'And when I sought the reason of their journey to Brighton they

Meredith's car outside his Church Hotel pub. Meredith never learnt to drive and his handy-man, Algy, is in the driving seat.

Meredith's name is seen on a cinema poster, advertising his training film. He would often make personal appearances at cinemas and theatres.

answered in a chorus, 'To see Billy Meredith, of course. What a marvel! Was there ever such a man; what a commentary upon the youngsters this digging up of the old fellow!'

'These men had no special interest in either Manchester City or Brighton – they had but a mind for Meredith, 'the old man called upon to show the young idea how it should be done'.

'And when I reached Brighton I hastened to find Meredith. Years had gone since we last chatted. Said he in a half-shy way, "This is a wonderful day for me, and I hope I will justify my selection. I think I will for I feel fine".'

And out he went, silver-haired, to be greeted by twenty-four thousand people packed into the Goldstone Ground.

In the excitement created by Meredith's selection, Brighton had almost been forgotten (perhaps this had been Mangnall's intention). Now they were overwhelmed and lost the match 5-1. The gamble had paid off, and Meredith had scored a goal.

In the second half he had taken on Brighton's left-back, darted past him and then lifted a centre into the goalmouth which the goalkeeper had fumbled and somehow palmed into the net.

The headline 'Bombshell at Brighton' did not seem unduly exaggerated. Afterwards Meredith said, 'I had a real hope that we would win but I didn't think we'd do it 5-1. It was our tactics that beat them.' As for his own performance, 'I feel quite alright ... our methods suited my style and I was never worried by the speed and vigour.'

Manchester was now completely caught up in this last Meredith saga. The *Topical Times* said: 'It reads like a romance but Billy Meredith is not made of ordinary stuff and the grey matter he has in his head belies his years to a degree and also makes us forget that Billy does less futile running about than any winger of today or yesterday. Pace, says Billy, counts for little – ball control and wisdom for everything.'

In the quarter-finals, City were to meet Cardiff, then approaching the peak of their First Division days. Seventy-six thousand spectators crammed into Maine Road that day to watch a 0-0 draw, and the *Manchester Guardian* tried to be objective about Meredith: 'There was great interest in Meredith's play. He is one of the Trojans, but he is also one of the veterans. He was as useful as any of the Manchester forwards but it is, all the same, a confession of weakness to play him. He performs as artistically as ever that strange feat of magnetising the ball round his toes in a half-circle and then running down the field to the goal-line with a ferocious half-back somehow kept always on the offside of him. He was only beaten once or twice all Saturday afternoon. The trouble is not that he cannot go for and fight for the ball as he did twenty years ago, but that, small blame to him, he just lacks that fragment of speed and strength that makes all the difference. It made all the difference on one occasion on Saturday between an excellent shot and a decisive goal. But Cardiff will not see on Wednesday any finer master of tactics or controller of the ball.'

And so it turned out. All Wales looked forward to the replay, for both sentimental as well as loyal club and national reasons, though there was some local scepticism as to Meredith's ability to achieve very much. The *Western Mail* correspondent wrote: 'I shall, apart from anything else, be particularly interested in the duel between the veteran Billy Meredith and the great Billy Hardy. Brilliant player though he has been, I think the Lancashire club have made a mistake in selecting the famous Welsh international. It will surprise me very much if Hardy does not succeed in 'boxing' him from the start, and thus reduce appreciably the effectiveness of the Manchester vanguard.'

But all such doubts were, once again, to be dispelled. Before another massive crowd, this time of fifty-five thousand, Meredith laid on the goal that knocked the powerful South Wales club out of the Cup.

After causing the Welsh crowd some heart-fluttering moments in the first half with some dashing runs and perceptive centres, he settled down to play probably his finest game for many years. Unfortunately for Cardiff, Hardy received an injury early in the game which reduced the overall efficiency of the defence, but, as one Welsh reporter admitted, 'in the wily veteran Meredith, Hardy met a winger who beat him more often than any other winger has done this season.'

Jimmy Broad, back now as City trainer, felt that it was Meredith's control of the ball that lifted him above all the other forwards: 'His superiority was due to the fact that he could control the light ball with comparative ease, whereas most of the other players were often beaten by it. On the hard, dusty ground, the ball bounced disconcertingly, but hardly once was the veteran deceived by it.'

In the second half, with the score sheet blank, Meredith fashioned the move that sent the Cardiff crowd home bitterly disappointed. That he had once been their greatest idol could have been of little comfort to them. Few would have savoured the trickery with which he set up the decisive score; indeed, many an older fan probably sensed a sinking feeling in the pit of the stomach as Meredith set off down the right-wing – they had seen it too many times in the past. The *Topical Times* described the goal: 'Keeping the ball at the end of his toes as surely as though he had it on a piece of string, the veteran glanced in his bird-like fashion to his left, as though he meant to pass

Famous five in training for the 1924 FA Cup semi-final against Newcastle. Each member of the forward line would end his career with more than 100 goals. Left to right: Billy Meredith, Frank Roberts, Tommy Browell, Horace Barnes, Tommy Johnson. Behind them stand Jimmy Broad (trainer) and Tommy Chorlton (assistant trainer).

in that direction. Blair saw this, and kept his position accordingly; but like a flash the forward darted ahead and leaving the back standing, as it were, he was able to go on and put in a centre which left the Cardiff goal at the mercy of Browell.

'Browell so soon as he had pushed the ball into the net rushed to Meredith to offer his praises; this and that Manchester player surrounded the grand old man for the goal which was designed to take their team to the last round but one of the competition was really his.

'And when the match was over and I was hurrying back to London, I bid adieu to the fifty-year old wonder. "See you at Wembley" said he, his weather-beaten face wreathed in smiles.'

City were in the semi-final. At that stage the possibility of Meredith appearing in a Cup Final at Wembley was, for Mancunian minds, incredible. And yet, just ninety minutes stood between the dream and the reality. For Meredith, suddenly playing with confidence and to great effect, the idea of a Wembley appearance must have kept him awake at nights. The opposition in the semi-final after all, was Newcastle United, who were now a far less powerful team than before the war, and certainly less of a hurdle than Cardiff. And Meredith had always played well against Newcastle sides over the years.

Meredith prepared by playing in another League game at Maine Road. On the Saturday prior to the semi-final, the 2-2 draw against Preston North End proved to be his last League appearance. In an undistinguished game, Meredith rarely touched the ball.

And something of the Preston match carried over into the semi-final. The enthusiasm and confidence that had grown ever since Meredith had joined the side swiftly drained away in a scrappy, disappointing semi-final played at St Andrew's, Birmingham. City suffered the disappointment of having a goal disallowed, and when Newcastle scrambled a goal in the second half it never looked likely that City would equalise. Newcastle played a holding game to perfection and City could not seem to mount a threatening attack all through the second half. The forwards simply tore along on lone forays, hoping to storm the black and white citadel single-handed. Meredith hardly received a pass all afternoon.

One report summed it up: 'The forwards were never a combined force and, although Roberts made one long dribble, they were not impressive individually. Many of the intended passes sent the ball to opponents. Meredith had many idle moments, although he clapped his hands to tell his colleagues that he was still on the field.'

Newcastle coasted to the final whistle, adding a second goal late in the game as many of the crowd were already making their way home. The fairy-tale had ended.

By one of football's strange twists of fate, Meredith had ended his career at City on the losing side against Newcastle, just as he had started it, thirty years before.

Billy Meredith, in his fiftieth year, prepares for the 1924 FA Cup semi-final.

MEREDITH TESTIMONIAL.

HIS RECORD:

WELSH INTERNATIONAL: 51.   GOALS SCORED: 15.

CHARITY: 400.   GOALS SCORED: 90.

MANCHESTER CITY: 789.   GOALS SCORED: 315.

ASSISTED IN RAISING **£50,000** FOR CHARITY.

10

Football's Grand Old Man

'If you should ever go to Manchester and would like to talk over times that are past, or should you wish to listen to the sagas of men and games of a generation that is gone, then call at the Stretford Road Hotel and meet the host Billy Meredith. You might find some little changes in the gallant Welshman of international repute above all others, but Billy is still the same eager champion of football that he was when his hair was not so grey. The same twinkle is in his blue eyes and the spirit of youth isn't gone from those legs and feet that so often took him on those defence-feared touchline dribbles.'
Topical Times, 31 January 1930.

With the Cup semi-final over, Billy Meredith's prodigious career had ended. It seemed a fitting finale – both controversial and bizarre. The publicity helped generate enthusiasm for a number of testimonial matches held in various parts of the kingdom the following year – the year of his official retirement. At Maine Road a Meredith XI met a combined Rangers and Celtic XI which included Alan Morton of Rangers and Jimmy McGrory of Celtic. Johnny McMahon, the ex-City full-back, and George Wall, the former Manchester United winger, ran the line, the latter, it was noted, calmly puffing a pipe.

The *Manchester Evening Chronicle* reporter wrote: 'Many old friendships were renewed at Maine Road on Wednesday night, and we all laughed at Meredith trying the old backheel to the half-back business with very little success.' One can be sure that Meredith would not have seen the joke.

In October, Colwyn Bay United put on a match, and in November

Manchester City 1925. An impromptu team group. Back row (l to r): Jimmy Broad: (trainer), Pringle, Sharp, Cookson, Ellwood, Fletcher, Wilson, T. Chorlton (assistant trainer), Wilf Wild (secretary). Front: Meredith, Roberts, Browell, Barnes, Johnson. Meredith's team mates now belonged to a completely different era from the one he had joined some thirty years earlier.

yet another Meredith team faced St Mirren, the Scottish Cup holders, at Anfield. Meredith's team that day was very much a North Wales old boys affair, with men from Chirk, Wrexham and Northwich Victoria – Dan 'Dicko' Davies, Dick Richards (who had appeared in the first Wembley FA Cup Final for West Ham) and Lloyd of Llanidloes, a keen salmon poacher, it was said.

Meredith continued to help City's coaching staff for a few more years, along with the indestructible Jimmy Broad; Meredith concerned himself more with the younger players, however, until in 1930 he moved to a new public house – the Stretford Road Hotel – and became a scout, helping Manchester United and Derby County among others.

In the early months of 1930, the *Topical Times* ran a series on former Cup heroes. Twenty-six years after Manchester City had brought the Cup to Manchester for the first time ('A triumph of youth for there

Meredith demonstrating his balance and style on the bowling green.

were but two players in the team who were more than twenty-two years of age') four of the famous eleven were dead: Ashworth, 'Snowball' Frost, 'Tabby' Booth and Sandy Turnbull. Three were abroad: Herbert Burgess and Tom Hynds were coaching in Italy and South America respectively, while Gillespie was an electrician in Montreal. George Livingstone was a trainer at Bradford City, Jack Hillman was a tobacconist, and Johnny McMahon was a successful publican in Manchester.

By contrast, of the United side now twenty-one years on from their great days at Crystal Palace, only Harry Moger, their giant goalkeeper, was dead. And only Alec Bell was still in football as a trainer – at Manchester City. Meanwhile, Charlie Roberts, Harold Halse and Jimmy Turnbull had all become prosperous businessmen; Hayes and Duckworth were publicans; George Stacey had returned to mining; and George Wall had found a comfortable job on Manchester docks.

By 1930, Billy Meredith had been a publican for fifteen years. He had just become tenant of the Stretford Road Hotel and was comfortably well-off, though by no means as wealthy as he might have been,

In 1934, Billy Gillespie returned from Canada for a holiday. Above, he is pictured at Billy's pub, the Stretford Road Hotel. They are joined by the seemingly indestructible Jimmy Broad, forty years after they were all in their prime at Hyde Road. From left, Jimmy Broad, Billy Gillespie, Mrs Gillespie, Stacey Lintott (Daily Mirror sports editor), and Meredith.

had he possessed the business acumen of his old United captain and union colleague, Charlie Roberts. As Meredith himself commented in 1919: 'I may have been a star footballer – but I have often thought that if I began life again I would try and get the loan of Carpentier's business manager.' (Georges Carpentier was one of boxing's greatest box office attractions).

Of all Meredith's colleagues from the great days, Roberts was probably the most successful in retirement. By the mid-1930s he had already established the basis for a thriving wholesale tobacco business, one that continues growing today. Meredith, on the other hand, was both unable and unwilling to devote himself wholly to business. Even the relatively undemanding role of publican never really suited him – he concentrated on cellar-work and talking over the bar to old friends, playing-colleagues and anyone who would lend an ear.

Meredith never had ambitions beyond the football field, never lost his fascination for the game, and never ceased hankering to get back on to the pitch and play. Like a precious possession that he had let fall into someone else's hands, football was a source of anxious concern to him and he suffered a mixture of heartbreak at its loss and jealousy of its new owners. Many retired players admit that once their playing days are over, they lose interest and even sympathy with the game, but Meredith could not resist its fatal attraction and he suffered because of it.

The five years between his final testimonial in 1925, and his move to the Stretford Road Hotel, had been happy and eventful ones, however. Unlike almost all his old colleagues, Meredith was a legend even before he had finished playing. As a consequence, much happened to him that could not have happened to, for instance, George Wall who was a dashing winger in his time and yet who finished his days working in the docks.

In 1926, for example, Meredith starred in a full-length feature film, playing himself as a football trainer. The film was widely distributed and was shown in picture houses in which Meredith himself had financial interests. The reviews were favourable: 'A British Sporting Picture I think most people will like,' wrote the *Topical Times* film critic, 'is *Ball of Fortune*. The somewhat complicated plot deals with the adventures of a young man who is swindled out of his money by relatives and relates how, in the course of his wanderings, he makes friends with Billy Meredith, the international footballer, under whose guidance he becomes a popular favourite in the sporting world. James Knight is very good as the hero and there is a capital football match which is bound to arouse enthusiasm.'

The *Kinematograph Weekly* felt that Meredith had played his part well, that the football scenes were good and that with 'popular sporting audiences, this picture will be a winner'.

Though quite obviously no classic – there is no trace of the film remaining save some 'still' photos – it was certainly a rarity. Somehow, despite the importance of football to British cultural history the marriage between it and that other potent form of mass entertainment, the cinema, has hardly ever been seriously attempted. Meredith, ever the entertainer, can be credited with playing a part in trying. Whatever its merits, the film was a success in Chirk where a packed village hall cheered whenever their most famous son appeared on the screen.

Box-office Angle.—Fair popular stunt picture.

The Ball of Fortune

Booth Grainge. British. Featuring Billy Meredith, James Knight, and Mabel Poulton. Six reels. Release not fixed.

Story.—Young Dick Heuish presents a favourite uncle with a cigarette-case as the latter is about to go abroad. Years elapse, and the uncle and his son are prosperous. Dick arrives ruined, and is badly treated by his relatives. It is soon evident they have annexed the money which should be his. Their plots against him land him into the police court, when he is befriended by a lawyer, who becomes his firm friend. He also wins the love of the magistrate's daughter. Another firm friend is Billy Meredith, the famous international footballer, and under his wing becomes himself an idol of the sporting world. Eventually the villains are unmasked, and after playing in a big match, Dick wins his bride.

A POPULAR type of British sporting picture, which possess all the ingredients for success.

Acting.—James Knight is capital as Dick, Mark Barker excellent as the lawyer, Mabel Poulton is not quite up to the form she has hitherto shown as the heroine. A capital little study of "vamp" comes from Dorothy Boyde, and many other parts are well played, notably by Geoffrey Partridge and Billy Meredith.

Production.—Hugh Croise has tackled his job well, and made a good deal out of a somewhat ordinary melodramatic story. Chief interest centres on the football scenes, and these are very good.

Settings and Photography.—The sets are adequate, without presenting anything new. The photography is good.

Box-office Angle.—With popular sporting audiences, this picture will be a winner.

Review of 'The Ball of Fortune' from the Kinematograph Weekly, *1926.*

It was not just Meredith's own adventures that continued to find their way into the newspapers after his retirement. His family were still newsworthy, too. In 1930 he appeared on the front page of the *Manchester Evening Chronicle* escorting his daughter Winnie to her wedding. Earlier that year Winnie had achieved fame of her own by winning the cup awarded by the *Dancing Times* at Blackpool, much to her proud father's delight. Always the strict Edwardian father, he had at first disapproved of her dancing in public but, fortunately for Winnie, she possessed some of her father's own stubborn determination and eventually she had won him over. Now twenty-four and strikingly beautiful, she was winning cups in true Meredithian fashion, just as she and her elder sister Lily had won awards and prizes at school for running.

Where athletics had been concerned, there had been no paternal reservations. Meredith trained his two girls to his own strict standards, had set them arduous schedules, timed them, rubbed them down and driven them on as he might have done had they been boys. Lily even managed to become Cheshire sprint champion.

That he had no son was a disappointment to him but, in many ways, it was probably a blessing. There could have been no other occupation but football for any son of Billy Meredith, and who but a genius could have measured up to the great man's awesome standards? He badgered his grandsons so relentlessly that they lost interest in the game as a profession. For a son, the pressures might have been overwhelming.

In the event he had to settle for a footballing son-in-law. Lily, his eldest daughter, married Charlie Pringle, a young Scot signed by Manchester City in 1920 from St Mirren. Meredith actually played with Pringle during his last few seasons at Maine Road and Pringle went on to a Cup Final appearance at Wembley in 1926 against Bolton. Later, he played an important role in the efforts to launch a third League club in the city – Manchester Central F.C. It was a venture in which Meredith also had a hand.

In 1929, a consortium of businessmen and local interested parties felt the time was right for a football club to fill the gap left by the removal of Manchester City westward to Maine Road. With football attendances booming, the attraction of reviving the old idea of using the massive Belle Vue stadium was tempting. Charlie Roberts, Johnny

Meredith playing in a charity match on the Chirk FC ground in the 1930s. Though well over fifty, he was still sending defenders the wrong way on the ground where he began his career.

McMahon and Meredith were all involved at the outset, Meredith on the coaching and talent-spotting side. A promising start was made, the club entering the Lancashire Combination. The management had high hopes of tapping local talent rather than spending money on established players – for a time Charlie Roberts' son played for

Central until his father, always the realist, told him he would do better to concentrate on the family business. But the ambitious scheme ran out of steam after just three years. In their second season, during which Charlie Pringle, his career revived, moved on to Bradford City, Central were runners-up in the Combination but could not gain entry to the Third Division North. By the time the club's affairs were being wound up, Billy Meredith had left the Gorton-Hyde Road area and, after a short, unsuccessful period in semi-retirement, he became tenant of the Stretford Road Hotel.

His swift return to the public-house business can be seen, in part, as testimony to his continuing restlessness and a reluctance to step out of the limelight. His new hotel, soon known in the area simply as 'Billy Meredith's', gave to him once more a personal platform from which he could deliver the definitive judgements, the provocative assessments of players, teams and tactics calculated, it often appeared, to keep the cauldron of controversy bubbling merrily down through the inter-war years.

Tactically, the game had altered a great deal since the Edwardian era. In particular, Meredith had played under an entirely different offside rule, the alteration of which in 1925 he had thoroughly disapproved: 'I fear him to have little or no liking for the new rule; maybe the secret is old-fashionedness. At any rate, he will have none of it and sees it as an emaciated thing, something that does not bring out the arts and graces of the game as did the old conditions,' wrote one reporter.

As the years rolled on, his sense of dislocation increased, particularly as those playing under the new rule felt that it rendered obsolete much of what veterans such as Meredith had to say about the 'modern' game. Needless to say, Meredith dismissed such opinions with contempt and consistently attacked what he felt was a gradual decline in standards: 'The new offside rule demands speed first, last and always ... The football enthusiast today is less tolerant towards players who weave dainty patterns; his praise is for the man who gets ahead. I am sorry that this should be so. The clever individual player is being crushed out to make way for the man who has less football craft but is credited with going full-speed ahead for goal. This sort of game wasn't encouraged in my time. We were brought up in the school when football science counted above everything. Mere speed

Meredith with the great Alex James (far right). Also pictured are Cardiff goalkeeper Sam Irvin (extreme left) and Welsh FA secretary Ted Robbins, who was a great battler for the cause of Welsh football and one of Meredith's best friends.

wasn't given a chance. . . If I were building a side, the clever player would play the big-drum. I would have no room for the bustler with nothing else to commend him. . .'

But Meredith was not building sides. Men like Herbert Chapman were, and the great Arsenal teams of the 1930s provided a perfect demonstration of Meredith's main point. Cliff Bastin and Joe Hulme, dashing, free-scoring, but by no means ball-playing wingers, were setting a fashion that, for good or ill, a thousand lesser players would find easier to imitate than Meredith's more 'dainty' style.

But it was not all scathing dismissals and 'golden' memories. While he had the security of the Stretford Road Hotel behind him, and numerous colleagues old and new with whom he could discuss the finer points of football until the early hours, he still had much to say that was positive.

His chief delight, of course, was to travel with the Welsh team, and he rarely missed an international match of any kind from the day he played his last game for Wales in 1920, right through until the mid-

1940s. Scores of Welsh players recall being wished good luck by Meredith on their international debuts. It became an unofficial initiation ceremony in itself.

Cliff Jones, the Wales and Tottenham Hotspur winger remembers: 'When I was playing for Swansea Boys in the English Schools Trophy Final against Manchester Boys at Maine Road in 1950, Billy Meredith came into the dressing room before the game to wish us good luck, which was very nice of him. He was certainly chewing his toothpick then. . .'

And Jimmy Murphy, another Welsh international, who later helped Matt Busby build, and rebuild, the great Manchester United sides of the 1950s and 1960s says, 'I met him in the dressing room at the Racecourse, Wrexham, in the early 1930s – it was my first Welsh cap – he introduced himself and wished me luck. After the war, when United played at Wembley, Billy loaned me his very old Cup Final medal to bring us luck. . .'

And the old longing to get out on to the pitch and lend a hand was strongest when it came to internationals. Dave Whitcomb, a West Bromwich half-back, recalls an occasion at the end of World War Two: 'We played Scotland at Hampden Park in a Victory international. . .

In 1947, a charity match was played for Billy at Glenceiriog, near Chirk. As part of the publicity for the game, Billy's photograph was hung on the gates of Chirk Castle.

We travelled up on a Tuesday as the match was on a Wednesday. At ten o'clock that night we only had ten players as Hughes, Dearson, and Edwards had gone to Germany with Birmingham City for a short tour and their plane was held up over there owing to the weather. The leg-pulling started. "Got your boots with you, Bill?", "Early to bed, Bill!", "Training in the morning, Bill?", and so on, with the other players all having a go at him. As it happened the three players turned up at three o'clock on the Wednesday morning. I think Billy was more sorry than glad, but he had his revenge on us as we lost the match and he said, "You wouldn't have lost it if I'd been out there with you".'

By now, Meredith was no longer tenant at the Stretford Road Hotel. He had retired in 1945 and gone to live with his daughter Winnie, his wife Ellen having died in 1933. He was now the Grand Old Man of Football, a permanent VIP. There were always seats for him at all the big games, though he was never happier than when allowed to settle in the corner of a dressing room, unobserved. He had little to say on such occasions, would simply sit with his hands deep in his pockets, chewing on his toothpick, totally absorbed in the hustle and bustle of pre-match preparations. At such times a stranger attempting to strike up a conversation was usually doomed to ignominious failure. Ceirog Williams, a radio reporter in the 1950s, recalls such an incident at the Racecourse Ground, Wrexham, after a Welsh international: 'There was this lone figure sitting and chewing on his toothpick. He had nothing to say, was very reticent. I ventured to ask if it was a toothpick or a quill in his mouth. He must have been aware of the controversy regarding what it was, and he just smiled and stuck out the point of his tongue, and it was a toothpick (or a match-stick).'

Eric Thornton, sports editor of the *Manchester Evening News* had an even harder task in 1947 when he took Meredith to the Cup Final of that year between Burnley and Charlton Athletic: 'It had looked to be a good idea and the arrangement was that I phoned the running report direct from my seat at the stadium, halted every few minutes to obtain his (Meredith's) considered opinion, and then pushed through three or four paragraphs under his name.

'We started alright, because when I first turned to him, he said, "Burnley are covering well, especially against the long ball, but Charlton are using it better". Good enough. That was spun out to

FOOTBALL ASSOCIATION CHALLENGE CUP - SEASON 1947-48

The Chairman and Directors of

MANCHESTER UNITED FOOTBALL CLUB LIMITED

request the pleasure of the company of

.... Wm Meredith Esq., ... XXXXX

at a

Cup-Final Dinner and Dance

*at the Connaught Rooms, Kingsway, London, on
Saturday, 24th April, 1948 at 7-0 for 7-30 p.m.*

R.S.V.P. to—
W. Crickmer, Secretary,
United Road, Manchester, 16
Not later than April 17th   Informal

three paragraphs, after which I resumed the move-by-move account. When another ten minutes had elapsed I turned to him again, but he said almost the same thing. So I asked him to give me some new point, and felt I'd got through to him because he picked up another tooth-pick. But on the half-hour, when I turned to him a third time, poor old Billy came out just the same – "Burnley are covering well. . .". So I let him go on enjoying the game, and added occasional paragraphs on his behalf because he obviously didn't feel in the mood for the unaccustomed role of sportswriter instead of player.'

Despite the fuss made of him on such occasions (and he was back at Wembley the next year as guest of honour when Manchester United beat Blackpool) and despite frequent radio appearances and celebrity dinners, Meredith became convinced as he approached his eighties that he was being neglected, even ignored by the football world to which he had once contributed so much. He quarrelled with Manchester City for reasons that were unclear, and when he spoke of the modern game it was generally with a disdain bordering on contempt.

Unfortunately his caustic comments were interpreted as bickering, as sour grapes – he was the typical old player who felt that the good old days were the best and that nothing modern players could do would ever match those high standards. All of which was unfortunate because Meredith had been pointing out faults in the English game

Meredith, with the modern FA Cup after Manchester United had won it in 1948. From left, Jimmy Delaney, Charlie Mitten and Allenby Chilton show the present trophy to the man who twice played in sides which won the previous Cup.

for many years, and with some justification. As far back as 1918 a journalist in the *Sporting Chronicle* had written: 'It has long been the opinion of the greatest wing-forward of all-time that our methods are all wrong. The system adopted by the majority of clubs has never been to his liking. His contention has always been that players in training get too much running and too little of the ball, but long before this stage is reached he considered that boys with a bent for fame are neglected. . .

'If you want good footballers, you must catch them young and you must train them properly. The common practice of putting a youngster into a pair of running pumps and setting him on sprinting exercises immediately he arrives must be altered. Often enough he never gets a real chance of showing his skill as a footballer.'

But he continued to be drawn into controversy of one kind or another – in a way, he had always thrived upon it. In an article on Stanley Matthews he wrote: 'I wonder how Stanley Matthews would get on if he were suddenly transported into soccer in the early 1900s? He would be given no time to stand still and entertain the crowds as he does today. "Straight into the tackle" were the orders defenders

Meredith was a regular broadcaster for years after he played his final game, and his opinions were widely sought.

played under in those days. If I had played like Matthews does, I should have been in hospital.'

Needless to say, the article drew the desired response: 'Mr Meredith, you make me sick with your bragging about how good you and your contemporaries were compared to present-day players...' wrote one indignant reader.

Those closest to him, particularly the many young boys he befriended, coached and advised during his last years, remember only his wry humour and unswerving insistence on the simple virtues of a game which, as he said at the end of his 1919 memoirs, 'was my only love, for it is a noble and manly game'. The concluding line of those same memoirs explains why he continued, right up to the end of his life, to derive so much pleasure from watching youngsters play: 'If I

Meredith meets Charlie Mitten and his daughter on the way to Wembley in 1948.

had to live my life again and possessed the power to decide my own destiny I would still wish to become a better footballer than I have ever been in the past'. In fact, he simply transferred his own genuine desire to go on improving his skills to the boys he met on his long and solitary walks through the parks and playing-fields of southern Manchester. G. Williams, who, like Meredith, lived in Withington in the late 1950s, remembers a typical incident. After watching Williams play in a junior match one morning Meredith asked for the boy's right football boot. The next day it was returned with a ball attached to the boot's toe by a cord some two feet long. Meredith had noticed a slight weakness in Williams' right foot and suggested he dribble the ball wherever he went, never letting the string tighten.

From this and countless other similar examples of the painstaking care and attention paid to the development of junior players, it is clear that Meredith's alleged jealousy of those in the professional game was as much a real concern with the shoddy preparation and groundless confidence of Football League players in their apparent superiority, as it was a natural resentment felt by one long past his prime for those just entering theirs.

One thing did, inevitably, continue to cause him heartaches – the problem of money. Once he had relinquished the Stretford Road

Hotel, he had little in the way of solid investments on which to fall back, and towards the end of his life he was almost destitute. The Players' Union, the PFA, whose meetings he had continued to attend until he was physically incapable of doing so, helped him with small donations; Manchester United contributed payments on a club house; there were even further small benefit matches held in Chirk. On the occasion of one of them, a large photograph of the great man was draped across the gates of the beautiful Chirk Castle. In the same year the Black Park Pit across the valley closed down. His past was fast disappearing.

The 1940s and 50s were a time when research into the game's history was practically non-existent, when football was careless of its heritage, there being no immediate financial gain to be had. With no club museums replete with cash to bid for them, his unique collection of medals and caps could only lie under his bed until, after his death, they were sold off cheaply to anonymous collectors. Television was then in its infancy and thus there was little opportunity for Meredith and his achievements to reach a wider audience perhaps through the sort of documentary his life and career deserved. And though there were one or two attempts, no-one seemed concerned enough to write a book about his career, the book he would so liked to have seen. Only current stars could guarantee the profits required; to the mass of football fans he was simply a name from a dim and distant past, a curiosity to be patronised on radio quiz shows; the man himself might just have been dead and buried for all football seemed to care.

There were some younger players, however, who would call in on him occasionally and pay their respects – certain of the Busby Babes from the mid-1950s like Tommy Taylor, Duncan Edwards.

But for those who had seen him play, who had played alongside him and who had survived with him from a world that now seemed as distant as a strange planet, Meredith remained their inspiration – the dazzling right-winger forever threading his way to the bye-line. He spent two spells in hospital in the mid-1950s before his death in 1958. When it was first announced in the evening papers that he was in hospital, letters poured in from all over the country, wishing him well, recalling old times, reminiscing.

Will Davies had played in the Combination League when Meredith had still been with Chirk: 'Yes Billy, you were my idol. Stanley Matthews and all those so-called footballers? Enough said. Your record puts them to shame.'

Fred Fenton remembered playing against Meredith and Ross for Gainsborough Trinity: 'I marvelled at your wonderful play that day.'

Jack Kirnon, eighty-four years old and a survivor of the 1901 Cup Final, wrote to him to wish him luck.

Joe Schofield, an original 'Outcast' and once Meredith's understudy at Manchester United, recalled: 'Remember when we struck? Yes, the powers-that-be are just as autocratic today as they were in those far-off days'.

Not only old players sent their best wishes; supporters were anxious to remind and thank him.

W. Downey had been at the Cup Final of 1904 and had seen him score the winning goal: 'I was then in the St Joseph's Boys' Band and we used to play music at the game before the kick-off.'

And Charles Appleyard, who remembered Meredith's first-ever game at City, wrote a letter that provides a clue perhaps to football's enduring hold on those who have watched the game when young, those 'men on the terraces' of Gordon Jeffrey's poem for whom:

> . . . *sometimes through the dullest play*
> *Something comes back from an earlier day*
> *A fleeting moment, a hint of grace*
> *Brings back a feeling, a time, a place. . .*

Appleyard told Meredith: 'I was pleased to see your photograph in the *Daily Herald* which was well described "The Daddy of them All". I remember your first match at Hyde Road and the special bill announcing that William Meredith of Chirk would partner Finnerhan, the star of City, never thinking his new partner would become City's star for a good many years. I am seventy-four, lived in Gorton in those days. I carry a cutting in my wallet with the heading, "The Greatest of Them All". Many people ask me if you compared with Stanley Matthews. I always say you did, for one reason, you didn't zig-zag all over the field, but straight down the touchline and woe betide any back that tried the offside trap – a grand centre from the goal-line on to Sandy Turnbull's head and the ball was in the net. . .'

Sporting RECORD

★★ No. 859 Week ending Sept. 11, 1954 4ᴰ

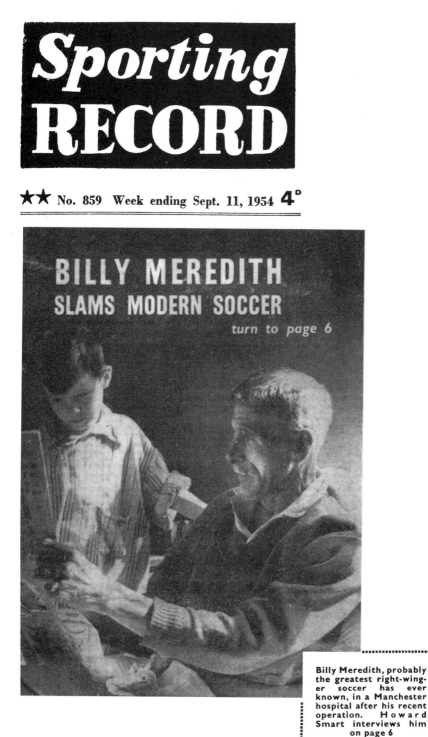

BILLY MEREDITH
SLAMS MODERN SOCCER

turn to page 6

Billy Meredith, probably the greatest right-winger soccer has ever known, in a Manchester hospital after his recent operation. H o w a r d Smart interviews him on page 6

Revenge is Sweet.

[Against Blackpool Meredith scored soon after he had been badly tripped.]

Appendix I:
Meredith's Playing Style

'In my day I could play on the right wing with only one eye. I only had to look ahead, not all around me. Once I had the ball I knew what was expected of me – to beat the wing-half and the full-back, take the ball down to the corner flag and centre. The other forwards knew my intentions and kept up with me.

'The plan was simple enough. It was also more direct. It made the game faster and more spectacular. A direct run to the corner and a lobbed ball was a more effective attack. Nowadays wingers cut in and you get a lot of bunched-up play and frenzied kicking around the goal mouth. The corners of the field are there to be used. We did use them when I was playing. Now you can almost pick mushrooms there.'
Extract from 'What I Think of Stanley Matthews' by Billy Meredith, Titbits 1947.

This brief analysis of Meredith's playing style and skills is set in the context of the once-traditional two full-backs, three half-backs, five forwards formation, an arrangement that continues, despite decades of experiment and upheaval, to influence the way we understand and look at the game.

At the turn of the century, the 2-3-5 formation suited to perfection the rules as they stood – in particular, the offside rule that required three of the defending team to be between an attacker and the goal when the latter received a forward pass. Thus the two full-backs could provide as much defensive cover as was necessary without the constant help of the centre-half who was much freer to move up with his fellow half-backs and link with the forward-line. The forward line, usually understood to be strung out along the field moving back and forth in unison, thus had the close support of a three man 'midfield'. And with so many players able to move forward into the opposition half, one can understand why certain sectors of the field became the almost exclusive territory of particular 'triangles' (winger, forward, half-back) and why there was so little roaming across the field in the fashion of modern isolated strikers. Territory was defined, as were duties and responsibilities; much as in the society of the day, everyone knew their place.

Nevertheless, there was a diversity of team styles and approaches. Indeed, the oldest controversy in the game concerning the best method of initiating attack (between the advocates of the swift and spectacular long aerial ball forward and the champions of the close-passing Scottish 'possession' game) raged long before the turn of the century. There was also a diversity of formations – deviations from the classic norm; play could never have been as rigid and as defined as the text-books would have us believe. Individual players with their differing abilities and skills inevitably 'broke the mould'. Billy Meredith in particular had a tremendous influence on the formation of the sides in which he played because he was so much more than simply a right-winger; and, just like other great players before and since, he transcended the limitations of the position in which he played.

First, we must start with the individual player, Meredith himself; and try to visualise his unique playing style.

Cartoons and pictures show him crouched and leaning over the ball, eyes usually fixed upon it. The cartoons exaggerated the stance, and his bandy legs (like a pair of calipers as one commentator remarked) but also showed his elbows jutting out, emphasising the crab-like style. His principal skill was, of course, his ball-control, a gift that never deserted him and which he was said to practise almost every day of his playing career and even beyond. He always kept the ball close, seemed at times to juggle with it, switching it from right foot to left in order to confuse opponents intent on dispossessing him. He fascinated friend and foe alike 'with that strange feat', as the *Manchester Guardian* writer put it in 1924, 'of magnetising the ball round his toes in a half-circle and then running down the field to the goal-line with a ferocious half-back kept always on the offside of him'.

The clever 'understandings' of two famous players – Donnachie and Meredith – which worked wonders last Saturday.

Meredith knew that his ball-control was the key to all he achieved in the game: 'Every fresh change in the placing of the men and every new circuit of the ball alters the positions of things to such an extent that the mind of the player requires to be continually open to adaptable ideas; but it is safe to say that command and control over the ball will solve many of the problems that present themselves. A player is always fairly master of the situation as long as he feels that he has the ball completely under control ... the knowledge that follows with the confidence that the ball is really in possession of the player will carry him through many difficulties. It is the motive power of his energies, the current showing him the shortest and best cut to goal.'

Dribbling the ball was not new, of course; indeed, in Meredith's heyday, at the turn of the century, it was almost regarded as a dying art, having been ousted in favour of 'combination' – the rapid passing and re-passing of the ball. In 1888, an observer wrote: 'The feature of modern association play is essentially the combination shown by a team. While each player has his place to keep, the field changes at each kick like a kaleidoscope, each player shifting his place to help a friend or check an adversary in the new position of the game.'

This emphasis on combination, James Walvin wrote, 'suited the style and attitudes and practices of working-class life. Working men

243

were accustomed to a crude division of labour to fulfil specific roles and functions; they were not expected to take upon themselves the individual responsibilities of their social superiors.' (*The People's Game*, Allen Lane 1975.)

In purely footballing terms, the popularity of passing stemmed from the fact that it was so effective and entertaining, so aesthetically satisfying – and to hold on to the ball when there was a man free was already being regarded in the 1890s by the masses of spectators as self-ish. 'Get rid of it!' had become a common cry from the terraces well before Meredith made his name. But Meredith's genius lay in the fact that, although he was a superb dribbler of the ball (and thus 'old-fashioned') he was also a brilliant passer. Though he could weave his way past lunging defenders, through flailing limbs, he made sure that at the end of his run he could pass the ball with breath-taking accuracy.

In the 1930s, Meredith was a golden memory in more ways than one: David Jack wrote, 'Centring as an art seems to be dying out. There is not a William Meredith in present-day football, for example. Meredith was a first-class winger in every way, but his crossing of the ball was *par excellence*, true in delivery and directed towards his colleagues with almost uncanny accuracy and strength. He rarely dropped a ball behind. The famous old Welsh international has thousands of admirers to this very day. They speak of his football – but they rave about his centring from the behind line as a natural screw delivered from the instep. . .'

In his own day, Meredith's combination of accuracy of crossing and close-dribbling was unique. Other great wingers – Bassett, Athersmith and Templeton – appeared to rely more on speed and power than control and accuracy. Bassett, England's winger when Meredith was in his youth, was said to release the ball as soon as he could after having beaten his man. He possessed a veritable 'box of tricks' to evade markers but, it was noted, 'he was averse to modern methods of passing and re-passing the ball'.

Athersmith, the man Meredith might have been challenging for a place in the England team, was similarly direct. Meredith himself noted of him: 'His chief points were his speed, his clever back-heel and splendid accuracy when serving up centres from corner-flags. He always had the foot on all his opponents and would kick the ball ahead and race for it. . .'. As Meredith put it, he was a 'speed merchant'.

ON THE SWERVE.

Our snapshot gives a good idea of Billy Meredith's characteristic swerve round an opponent. Verrill's desperate attempts to get at him at Middlesbrough on Saturday caused great amusement. Meredith was repeatedly cheered for clever play.

A full-back lunges at Billy Meredith but the Welsh wizard is already swerving past the defender.

Templeton, the flying Scot, was also fast, too fast for his colleagues at times, but Meredith noted, 'Strange to say, Templeton never seemed to get the knack of swerving in towards the centre while on the run, to have a crack for himself. . .'

Which brings us to the third facet which set Meredith finally apart from his wing-playing fraternity – his prodigious goal-scoring. As Meredith said: 'Every player who wishes to become an expert at the game must have more than one string to his bow. It is the man who adapts himself to the altered position and situations with new and fresh ideas that succeeds in these strenuously contested football days.'

As we have seen, as a youth for Chirk and Northwich Victoria, Meredith scored heavily, often playing at centre-forward. He continued to score literally hundreds of goals for Manchester City when he was in his athletic prime, between the ages of twenty and thirty – and he scored them by dint of hard, accurate, often long-range shooting. He would cut inside having beaten his marker out on the touchline, and shoot across the face of the goal. As he wrote in his memoirs, when talking of his second season with Manchester City: 'At that time I depended upon getting in a cross-shot from a spot about ten yards from the corner flag. I was always working for this position and never failed to shoot at goal when I got it. . .'

He was also adept at dashing in to meet crosses from the left wing and volleying into goal. And he was an accomplished penalty-taker. Thus, as a winger he could be compared to the greatest of his day and of any other day. But he was more than just a winger. He was a forward in the broadest sense, a creator and a scorer, as well as a supreme entertainer.

Today, there is a tendency to play down such virtuosity by suggesting that players like Meredith had fewer problems to overcome where organised defences were concerned. Inevitably, however, all is relative. Meredith himself, when commenting on Stanley Matthews' play, would say that the latter would never have been allowed to dwell on the ball so long in his, Meredith's, day; that full-backs appeared to give Matthews time and space in which to play the ball. It is certain that Meredith, though he might not have found himself boxed in by three or even four players, would have had much more in the way of physical contact to contend with than Matthews – shoulder-charging in particular. There are numerous reports of Meredith being bowled over, knocked into the hoardings around the grounds.

Yet there is still plenty of evidence to suggest that measures were taken to crowd him out, that once he had beaten the full-back, or half-back, the way ahead was not always clear. Meredith wrote: 'Frequently the centre-half will execute a sort of flanking movement while the full-back will operate on the touchline. Here we have something like a complete enveloping manoeuvre on the part of the opposing side and it will be with such situations facing one that the real merits of the player are tested to the utmost. . .'

Thus, contrary to the accepted image of Edwardian football – of men sticking rigidly to their positions – defence and full-backs did play as units combining with one another, backing one another up and even resorting to man-to-man marking when the occasion demanded it. As a winger, Meredith could normally expect to be watched by the opposing wing-half whose job it was to cut out passes to Meredith from his inside partners, or to dispossess Meredith before he could pick up pace. But once clear of the half-back, the full-back and the centre-half would be waiting. Often where Meredith was concerned, man-to-man marking was seen to be the only way of limiting the damage he could cause. We have seen how Evelyn Lintott performed this task so effectively for England.

Interestingly, it was often players from Manchester City's closest rivals, Newton Heath, who were most successful in the early days – men who would have had most opportunities to study him at close quarters, playing locally in charity and benefit matches; the majority of players would only have seen him once or twice a season, although there were others. Meredith recalled a match against Bolton Wanderers in the semi-final of the Lancashire Cup: 'I never remember feeling so exhausted as I did after that game. I was up against Scotchbrooke and from start to finish he let me know it. He certainly didn't consider my feelings that day and when next we met I'm afraid I did not thrust out the glad hand to him. With a smile he gave me a smack on the shoulder and said, "Not bearing any malice, Billy, are you? Bet I can make you smile in no half time. Thought I was a trifle rude to you that day, eh? Never mind. You'll be glad to know that, thanks to you, I got my wages raised a pound a week after that match. Wish you weren't teetotal, for then we could celebrate the occasion in style."

'Of course I felt flattered that his success in acting as policeman to me was considered valuable, but even as I smiled and congratulated him I couldn't help thinking of some of the hard knocks I had to take that day.'

On this very subject of close-marking, Tom Maley, the Manchester City manager in 1903, had this to say when assessing Meredith in relation to Bassett: 'Bassett was less temperamental. Bassett was the light sparkling poetry of motion. Meredith, though not a moody player, does reflect his mind's workings occasionally as witness when the proposition set doesn't follow the orthodox lines. You know what I mean, good reader. I mean when the Wizard Welsh William is up against some imperturbable knockout who won't leave him . . . like the Bradford half-back Lintott for whom Meredith required a piece of

Hands on hips, Meredith (fifth from left) watches the goalmouth action.

string so that they might be locked together! No, Meredith is not temperamental exactly, but he doesn't like, nor yet does he thrive under, conditions like the for-going... Like Bassett, Meredith is the poetry in motion, but it is of the serious, tragic order...

A close marker, it seemed, was the key to stopping Meredith. 'Argus Junior' in the Birmingham *Sports Argus* in 1905 felt that Meredith could often be reduced to being 'as helpless as a ship without a rudder, a confirmed smoker without a match'. He felt that Turnbull was more of a loss to City (at the time of the suspensions), adding, 'I do not wish to decry Meredith. I have seen him play many brilliant games, but I have also watched him (when) he has shipwrecked the whole forward-line; for they have waited in vain for those sleuth-hound dashes along the touch-streak and those lightning centres which capped the runs and nearly always spelt goals. William Meredith is a man of one style. I admit it is a graceful and exhilarating and generally look-out-some-thing's-going-to-happen sort of style, but when the smart half-back who understands Meredith's bland and peculiar ways is told off to act as policeman to the "flying Welshman", it's all England to a hayseed, that William Meredith is like the man who fell out of the balloon – he's not "in it".'

Pat Finnerhan (left) and George Livingstone were just two of the players who fetched and carried for Meredith.

Meredith was therefore, quite literally, a marked man. And it was here that his various partners down the years were so crucial to his success.

Meredith could never be criticised for losing his appetite for the game and in particular for the ball. It was another of his hallmarks that he was forever anxious to be involved – rarely, if ever, was he known to 'hide' on the field. Thus he needed men in close proximity to him who would dedicate themselves to fetch and carry for him, men like Pat Finnerhan, 'Stockport' Smith, Jimmy Ross, Jimmy Bannister, George Livingstone, Joe Picken and Harold Halse. To be the perfect partner for Meredith, one had to be tough, unselfish and shrewd; it is an interesting fact that few of Meredith's immediate inside partners scored goals. Only Harold Halse was primarily a goalscorer and significantly the partnership between the two was never a happy one. By contrast the inside-left (usually, it must be said, Sandy Turnbull) scored heavily, and usually from Meredith's passes. Without a reliable partner Meredith could very often be stranded in a game, particularly in the later years when his physical powers were on the wane, preventing him from going in search of the ball himself.

Meredith himself never failed to pay tribute to his partners, and he was wise enough to ensure that when he moved to Manchester United, the men most vital to his success – Turnbull, Bannister, and later Livingstone – went with him.

But not only were his inside-right partners of crucial importance to his success – his wing-halves also had a vital role to play. As we have seen, this was the period of the wing-triangles consisting of winger, half-back and inside forward combining, interpassing closely as they advanced on goal. In both the Manchester Cup-winning sides Meredith had skilful, hard-working half-backs behind him. For City there was Sammy Frost – a terrier of a tackler, a supreme 'ball-winner'. For Manchester United there was Dick Duckworth, a more skilful player than Frost and quite capable of going forward with the ball to act as a sixth forward, and part of a famous half-back line.

Meredith's great good fortune was that, throughout his long career – almost thirty years at the highest level – his partners remained with him for considerable periods of time. The understanding he built up with men like Bannister, Livingstone and Turnbull was able to develop until it was almost instinctive. Thus, Jimmy Bannister played alongside him for Manchester United and City for almost seven years, George Livingstone for nine years, and Sandy Turnbull in both inside-forward positions, for almost thirteen years. That other key position in the forward line to which Meredith delivered many of his passes – centre-forward – was dominated by just three men for the majority of his career: Gillespie was at City for eight years, while Jimmy Turnbull and Enoch West shared the position at Manchester United for another eight.

Meredith was indisputably the star, but his lieutenants were loyal, talented and of long-standing, and must be taken into consideration when assessing the Welshman's incredible career.

Appendix II:
Meredith's Statistics

The statistics of Billy Meredith's career have sometimes proved something of a puzzle, due as much to Meredith's own eccentric method of compiling them as to the erratic and unreliable sources of such figures around the turn of the century.

His international career provided the first major mistake, compounded by the Welsh FA in 1922 when it awarded Meredith a trophy for winning over fifty caps. He had in fact won forty-eight official caps, an extra three Welsh appearances being in Victory internationals. And until the end of his life, he persisted in claiming three caps for his first season in international football (1895-6), even though he had quite definitely missed the last match against Scotland, having been required to play for his club instead.

Where his League and Cup appearances are concerned, and the goals he scored in them, an even greater disparity appears to exist between modern statisticians and Meredith's own record. In 1925, in his final season, a benefit programme listed the grand total of his games played and goals scored, figures provided by Meredith himself. In all, he claimed to have played 857 League games – 554 for City and 303 for United. As for goals, he claimed 281 – 236 for City and 45 for United. Modern statisticians have, however, only managed to account for 670 League appearances in all, and only 181 goals. . . Why such a dramatic difference?

It cannot be that Meredith included charity and benefit matches in his total because, the same 1925 programme states '. . . he has played in 400 matches in this cause for the benefit of other players, and

The following tabulated story tells the tale of what Meredith deserves of his fellows :—

CITY. Season	League matches played	League goals scored	Cup Ties played	Cup Tie goals scored
1894-5	22	16	8	3
1895-6	30	20	10	4
1896-7	30	24	12	4
1897-8	30	20	10	5
1898-9	33	36	15	5
1899-1900	34	16	12	4
1900-1	34	12	8	3
1901-2	33	13	10	9
1902-3	34	24	6	4
1903-4	33	11	14	5
1904-5	34	12	12	3
1915-16	36	6	—	—
1916-17	36	4	—	—
1917-18	36	4	—	—
1918-19	36	9	—	—
1919-20	17	4	—	—
1921-22	40	4	3	1
1922-23	10	1	2	—
1923-24	5	—	3	—
1924-25	1	—	7	1
Total	551	236	132	51

UNITED. Season	League matches played	League goals scored	Cup Ties played	Cup Tie goals scored
1906-7	16	5	2	1
1907-8	37	10	4	—
1908-9	34	10	7	2
1909-10	31	6	1	—
1910-11	35	6	3	—
1911-12	35	3	6	1
1912-13	22	2	5	1
1913-14	34	2	1	—
1914-15	26	—	1	—
1919-20	19	2	2	—
1920-21	14	1	2	—
Total	303	45	34	5
Grand aggregate	857	281	166	56

Club	Season	League		Int'nls	
		Gms	Gls	Gms	Gls
Manchester City	1894-95	18	12	2	
	1895-96	29	11	2	2
	1896-97	28	11	3	2
	1897-98	30	14	2	
	1898-99	33	29	1	
	1899-1900	33	11	2	2
	1900-01	34	6	2	
	1901-02	33	7	2	
	1902-03	34	25	3	
	1903-04	34	9	1	
	1904-05	33	11	2	1
	1905-06*				
Manchester United	1906-07	16	5	3	1
	1907-08	37	10	2	
	1908-09	34		3	
	1909-10	31	5	3	1
	1910-11	35	5	3	
	1911-12	35	3	3	
	1912-13	22	2	3	1
	1913-14	34	2	3	
	1914-15	26			
	1919-20	19	2	3	
	1920-21	14	1		
Manchester City	1921-22	25			
	1922-23	1			
	1923-24	2			
Total		670	181	48	10

*no recorded appearances in season 1905-06

Meredith's own statistical record (top) reproduced from his 1925 Benefit Match programme, differs greatly from those compiled by modern statisticians.

254

scored 90 goals. Moreover he has appeared in 84 friendly matches and scored 28 goals. . .'

What have been left out of modern statistics, however, are the War Leagues. Meredith played almost continuously for City throughout World War One and claimed 144 appearances, and 23 goals. He also credited himself with 17 further appearances for City in 1919-20 – a real puzzle, for he was registered to play for no club during the first half of that season, and returned in January 1920, to play for Manchester United.

For the rest of the outstanding games, some 26 in all, it seems that in the post-war years, he lumped in any 'official' appearance for City, be it Central League or friendly, and for a man approaching fifty years of age, who can blame him? Before 1903, the difference between Meredith and the modern statisticians is some eight games, and these could well be matches that Meredith was not down to play in, but in which he did, in fact, appear.

Thus Meredith's own record reflects more accurately the number of games he played. Where goals are concerned, the problem is more intractable. Once again, Meredith must have the advantage – after all, he was actually there – and was one of the few men to take an interest in facts and figures. The modern researcher has to rely on match reports for the most part, and these are notoriously unreliable. However, as we have seen, Meredith did have a tendency to credit himself with goals that he felt were morally his, even though he had not applied the final touch.

When his unofficial appearances are included, we can see that Meredith played an incredible number of football matches – in almost twenty seasons, broken only by his enforced rest in 1905-6, he played in almost 1,600 games of one kind or another, 80 per season. And this does not include his seasons with Chirk and Northwich Victoria in the years 1890-94. With hardly a serious injury to speak of, it must be regarded as an incredible record.

Bibliography

Reid, W. *The Story of the Hearts,* Heart of Midlothian FC, 1925.

The Book of Football, Amalgamated Press, 1906.

Walvin, James *The People's Game*, Allen Lane, 1975.

Gibson and Pickford *Association Football and the Men Who Made It*, Caxton, 1906.

Jack, David *Soccer*, Putnam, 1934.

Corrigan, Peter *100 Years of Welsh Soccer*, Welsh Brewers, 1976.

Mason, Tony *Association Football and English Society 1863-1915*, Harvester Press, 1980.

Johnson, Fred *The History of Manchester City Football Club*, Holt Publishing, 1930.

Catton, Jimmy *Wickets and Goals*, Chapman and Hall, 1926.

Green, Geoffrey *There's Only One United*, Hodder and Stoughton, 1978.

Lerry, G.G. *The Collieries of Denbighshire*, Minshalls, Thomson & Co, Wrexham.

Young, Percy *An Appreciation of Football*, Dobson, 1951.

Young, Percy *Manchester United*, Heinemann, 1960.

Thornton, Eric *Manchester City – Meredith to Mercer and the FA Cup*, Hale, 1969.

Sharpe, Ivan *40 Years in Football*, Hutchinson, 1954.

Cowen, Frank *A History of Chesters Brewery Company*.

Newspapers etc.

Athletic News, Birmingham Sports-Argus, Bolton Cricket and Football Field, Border Counties Advertiser, Daily Dispatch, Daily Sketch, Empire News, Football Chat, Kinematograph Weekly, Manchester Evening Chronicle, Manchester Evening News, Manchester Football News, Manchester Guardian, Newcastle Football Leader, Newcastle Football Mail, News of the World, Reynold's News, Saturday Post, Sporting Chronicle, Thompson's Weekly News, Umpire, Western Mail, Windsor Magazine, Wrexham Leader, Manchester Official Programme, Manchester City Programme and Manchester United Programme.

Index